MAXIMIZE YOUR LIFE
PLANNER

THIS PLANNER IS FULL OF AWESOMENESS
AND VERY IMPORTANT TO ME

IF FOUND, PLEASE RETURN TO:

_____

_____

_____

_____

_____

REWARD:

_____

www.MaximizeYourLifePlanner.com

A **MAXIMIZE YOUR LIFESTYLE** RESOURCE

MARK 9:23

CONGRATS ON YOUR **MAXIMIZE YOUR LIFE PLANNER!**

The **Maximize Your Life Planner** is an effective tool for staying organized and on track with your goals. Here are a few reasons why having this written planner can be beneficial:

- **HELPS PRIORITIZE TASKS AND SCHEDULE:** Allows you to see all of your tasks and appointments in one place, making it easier to prioritize what needs to be done and when.

- **INCREASES PRODUCTIVITY AND FOCUS:** You can focus on one task at a time, instead of feeling overwhelmed by all the things you need to do. It also helps you to avoid procrastination, since you can see the deadlines for each task.

- **HELPS WITH GOAL SETTING:** Allows you to easily track your progress towards your goals and make adjustments as needed.

- **PROVIDES A SENSE OF ACCOMPLISHMENT:** Crossing off completed tasks or seeing the progress you've made towards your goals can give you a sense of accomplishment and motivation to keep going.

- **HELPS WITH REFLECTION:** Reviewing your planner regularly can help you reflect on your accomplishments, challenges, and areas for improvement.

- **INCREASES MEMORY RETENTION:** Writing things down helps with memory retention and helps you to remember important things you need to do.

- **VERSATILE:** This planner can be used for both your personal and professional life, scheduling work meetings, appointments, personal goals, to-do lists, deadlines, etc.

This planner is a great way to stay organized, focused, and motivated. If used with intention, it can help you achieve your goals and create the best life possible.

THE **GREAT EIGHT** 8 STEPS TO HELP MAXIMIZE YOUR LIFE

1. **SET CLEAR GOALS:** Identify what you want to achieve in different areas of your life, such as your faith, family, field (work or business), finances, fitness, friends, and fun. Break down these goals into smaller, more manageable steps and create a plan to achieve them.

2. **PRIORITIZE SELF-CARE:** Make time for yourself to rest and recharge. This includes getting enough sleep, eating well, exercising, and doing things that make you happy. Taking care of yourself will help you be more productive and fulfilled.

3. **CULTIVATE POSITIVE RELATIONSHIPS:** Surround yourself with people who lift you up, support you, and bring you joy. Invest in and be intentional with your relationships, so you can build a strong support system over time.

4. **LEARN AND GROW:** Keep learning and challenging yourself. Take classes, read books, listen to audios, attend workshops, and/or seek out mentors. Constantly learning new things will help you stay sharp and motivated.

5. **GIVE TO YOUR COMMUNITY:** Helping others can be incredibly rewarding and fulfilling. Giving to your community through volunteer work, supporting a cause you care about, or mentoring someone who reminds you of where you once were, can make a huge impact!

6. **BE PRESENT:** Practice mindfulness and focus on being present in the moment. Avoid getting caught up in regrets about the past or worries about the future. Live in the now.

7. **REFLECT AND EVALUATE:** Reflect on your life regularly, and evaluate what's working and what's not. Reflect on your progress and make any necessary adjustments. Live and Learn.

8. **BE ADAPTABLE AND FLEXIBLE:** Be open to change and be willing to adjust your plans as needed. Life is unpredictable and sometimes things don't go as planned. Be ready to adapt, evolve, and grow.

Remember, the most important thing is to focus on what is important to you... what makes you happy and fulfilled. These are some simple steps you can tailor to your specific needs and goals, which will lead to you creating the best life possible.

THE **DIFFERENT PARTS** OF THIS PLANNER

- ## CALENDAR OVERVIEW:
  Complete yearly calendar to reference your dates and plan your days well in advance.

- ## MONTHLY OVERVIEW:
  Having a plan for the month can help you prioritize tasks, set achievable goals, and make better use of your time. Utilize the side sections, "What Worked Last month?", "What Could Be Improved?", and "This Month's Goal/Focus", to create momentum and growth month after month. This is also the section to track your birthdays, important dates, places to go, and people to see. Lastly, at the end of each month, journal any highlights, reflection, and/or breakthroughs you've experienced. Overall, planning your month in advance can help you be more productive, organized, and focused.

- ## 10 BEFORE 10 GRATITUDE LIST:
  Starting your day with gratitude will help you focus on the good things in your life, rather than dwelling on negative thoughts or stressors. At the same time, this practice will set a positive tone for the rest of the day. Having an attitude of gratitude has been shown to have a number of benefits for mental and physical health... such as reducing symptoms of depression and anxiety, improving sleep, increasing feelings of happiness and contentment, and deeper, more satisfying personal relationships. Additionally, starting the day with gratitude can help you build a more resilient mindset and approach to challenges. Use this section to write 10 things by 10am you are grateful for.

  Here are a few EXAMPLES of things you can add to your gratitude list:

  - The roof over your head
  - Your the ability to wake up and start a new day
  - A warm bed to sleep in
  - The people in your life who love and support you
  - Your health
  - The delicious food to fuel your day
  - The opportunity to learn and grow
  - The freedom to pursue your passions and interests
  - The beauty of nature around you
  - The small things that bring you joy

  The most important thing is to focus on what you are grateful for in your own life. It could be anything big or small, personal to you.

Date: _3/21/23_
1. Coffee w/ my wife
2. Great workout
3. Waking up!
4. Family & Friends
5. Beautiful day today
6. New Customer
7. My upcoming trip!
8. Awesome jog
9. Conversation w/my kids
10. Promotion = More $$$

MAXIMIZE YOUR LIFE P L A N N E R

THE **DIFFERENT PARTS** OF THIS PLANNER (CONTINUED)

- ## WEEKLY OVERVIEW:

  Seeing a clear path to start your week can give you the motivation you need to stay focused and productive.

  1. Weekly and Daily Goals / Focus
  2. Weekly Stop / Start / Continue
  3. Quote of the Week
  4. Declaration of the Week
     (with space to write your own!)
  5. Personal and Work To-Do List
  6. Follow Up List for prospects / clients
  7. 20-hours of 30 minute slots to schedule
     (5am to 1am)
  8. Habit Tracker
     (with space to add your own habits!)
  9. Thoughts / Ideas / Visions / Dreams

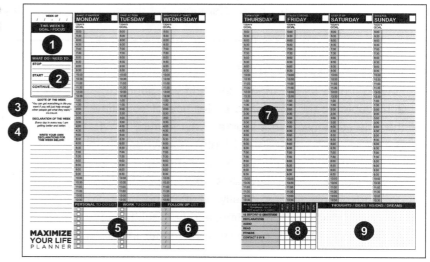

- ## CONTACT 5 BY 5:
  (Inside Your Habit Tracker)

  Cultivating positive relationships is one of the keys to maximizing your life and building a strong support system. Because of this, we encourage you to create a habit of contacting at least 5 people (friends, family, prospects, clients, follow ups, etc) before 5pm. Focus on a new 5 every day. Either make a new contact or reach out to someone you haven't spoken to in a while. Making new connections, as well as maintain current ones, is important for a variety of reasons: Career Advancement, Support System, Collaboration, Access to Resources, and Diverse Perspectives. Networking is a vital part of personal and professional development, and can have a significant impact on your ability to achieve your goals.

- ## MAXIMIZE YOUR DAY:
  (Your Daily Schedule is divided into 3 sections utilizing the grayed out area)

  Everyone has 24-hours in a day, but not everyone treats those 24-hours the same. Every minute of your day is either spent moving towards or away from the dreams God put on your heart. By viewing 24-hours as three days in one, you not only maximize your time, but also become three times more productive than the average person. Take your typical daily hours and divide it by three.

  FOR EXAMPLE:

  If your day is typically from 6am until midnight... Day 1 is 6am to 12pm. Day 2 is 12pm to 6pm. Day 3 is 6pm to 12am.

  While the average person has seven days in one week, you're developing a habit to maximize your days, which leads to 21 days in one week... and over 1000 days in a 365-day year.

THE 7 F's of LIFE (Faith, Family, Field, Finances, Fitness, Friends, and Fun)

Score each element for how you feel in your current state on a scale of 1 – 10. Rate yourself with 1 being very poor and 10 being outstanding. Even if you have done this before, we suggest reflecting and evaluating your score at least every six months for the rest of your life. The goal is to work towards becoming wellrounded which leads to a more fulfilled life.

	FIRST 6-MONTHS	SECOND 6-MONTHS

FAITH:
Personally connected to a higher power or purpose

Plugged into a community based on that power or purpose

Talking with others about your faith or purpose

TOTAL:

TOTAL ÷ 3 =

FAMILY:
The relationship with your spouse or significant other

The relationship with your kids or dependents

The level of family time

TOTAL:

TOTAL ÷ 3 =

FIELD:
How you feel about your career or business

Your commitment to personal/professional development

The level to which your field provides for you

TOTAL:

TOTAL ÷ 3 =

FINANCES:
Your level of debt (10 = out of debt)

Your level of a 6-12 month emergency fund (10 = complete)

Your level of investments / savings

TOTAL:

TOTAL ÷ 3 =

FITNESS:
Your level of exercise

Your commitment to nutrition

Your level of satisfaction on your sleep

TOTAL:

TOTAL ÷ 3 =

FRIENDS:
The quality of your friendships

The quantity of meaningful friendships

Your serving to those relationships

TOTAL:

TOTAL ÷ 3 =

FUN:
The activities you participate in

The enjoyment you get from them

Trying new things

TOTAL:

TOTAL ÷ 3 =

EXAMPLE

FIRST 6-MONTHS
DATE: _____

SECOND 6-MONTHS
DATE: _____

Now add up the TOTAL of each column and DIVIDE that number by 3. This will give you your personal score for that particular spoke on the wheel. Mark that number for each spoke on the wheel provided above, and connect the dots as illustrated in the EXAMPLE. What does your Wheel of Life look like? Is it round? Do you have flat spots? Do you have several spokes that need improvement? **Redo this exercise 6 months from now.**

GETTING CLEAR WITH THE 7 F's of LIFE

FAITH:
What role does your faith play in your life? _____
_____

Do you feel personally connected to a higher power or purpose? ☐ Yes ☐ No
Do you plug into a community based on that power or purpose? ☐ Yes ☐ No

FAMILY:
How important is family to you? _____
_____

What do you do to maintain strong relationships with them? _____
_____

FIELD:
What do you see as your career / business path? _____
What steps are you taking to achieve your goals and grow within that field?_____
_____

FINANCES:
What strategies do you use to manage your finances?_____
_____

What is your approach to tithing, saving, and investing?_____
_____

FITNESS:
How do you prioritize fitness in your daily life?_____
_____

What methods do you use to stay active?_____
_____

FRIENDS:
What value do you place on friendship?_____
_____

What steps do you take to cultivate strong relationships with others?_____
_____

FUN:
What do you consider to be fun activities? _____
_____

What do you enjoy doing in your free time? _____
_____

GETTING CLEAR WITH YOUR GOAL

LAST YEAR

What lessons did you learn from last year? _____
_____
_____
_____
_____
_____
_____

How can you apply the above lessons to this year? _____
_____
_____
_____
_____
_____
_____
_____

What do you want to achieve this year? _____
_____
_____
_____
_____
_____
_____

RETURN IN 6 MONTHS (DATE: _____)

What worked well in the last 6 months? _____
_____
_____
_____
_____
_____
_____

What could be improved in the next 6 months? _____
_____
_____
_____
_____
_____

How would you like to end the year? _____
_____
_____
_____

2023

JANUARY
M	T	W	T	F	S	S
						1
2	3	4	5	6	7	8
9	10	11	12	13	14	15
16	17	18	19	20	21	22
23	24	25	26	27	28	29
30	31					

FEBRUARY
M	T	W	T	F	S	S
		1	2	3	4	5
6	7	8	9	10	11	12
13	14	15	16	17	18	19
20	21	22	23	24	25	26
27	28					

MARCH
M	T	W	T	F	S	S
		1	2	3	4	5
6	7	8	9	10	11	12
13	14	15	16	17	18	19
20	21	22	23	24	25	26
27	28	29	30	31		

APRIL
M	T	W	T	F	S	S
					1	2
3	4	5	6	7	8	9
10	11	12	13	14	15	16
17	18	19	20	21	22	23
24	25	26	27	28	29	30

MAY
M	T	W	T	F	S	S
1	2	3	4	5	6	7
8	9	10	11	12	13	14
15	16	17	18	19	20	21
22	23	24	25	26	27	28
29	30	31				

JUNE
M	T	W	T	F	S	S
			1	2	3	4
5	6	7	8	9	10	11
12	13	14	15	16	17	18
19	20	21	22	23	24	25
26	27	28	29	30		

JULY
M	T	W	T	F	S	S
					1	2
3	4	5	6	7	8	9
10	11	12	13	14	15	16
17	18	19	20	21	22	23
24	25	26	27	28	29	30
31						

AUGUST
M	T	W	T	F	S	S
	1	2	3	4	5	6
7	8	9	10	11	12	13
14	15	16	17	18	19	20
21	22	23	24	25	26	27
28	29	30	31			

SEPTEMBER
M	T	W	T	F	S	S
				1	2	3
4	5	6	7	8	9	10
11	12	13	14	15	16	17
18	19	20	21	22	23	24
25	26	27	28	29	30	

OCTOBER
M	T	W	T	F	S	S
						1
2	3	4	5	6	7	8
9	10	11	12	13	14	15
16	17	18	19	20	21	22
23	24	25	26	27	28	29
30	31					

NOVEMBER
M	T	W	T	F	S	S
		1	2	3	4	5
6	7	8	9	10	11	12
13	14	15	16	17	18	19
20	21	22	23	24	25	26
27	28	29	30			

DECEMBER
M	T	W	T	F	S	S
				1	2	3
4	5	6	7	8	9	10
11	12	13	14	15	16	17
18	19	20	21	22	23	24
25	26	27	28	29	30	31

2024

JANUARY
M	T	W	T	F	S	S
1	2	3	4	5	6	7
8	9	10	11	12	13	14
15	16	17	18	19	20	21
22	23	24	25	26	27	28
29	30	31				

FEBRUARY
M	T	W	T	F	S	S
			1	2	3	4
5	6	7	8	9	10	11
12	13	14	15	16	17	18
19	20	21	22	23	24	25
26	27	28	29			

MARCH
M	T	W	T	F	S	S
				1	2	3
4	5	6	7	8	9	10
11	12	13	14	15	16	17
18	19	20	21	22	23	24
25	26	27	28	29	30	31

APRIL
M	T	W	T	F	S	S
1	2	3	4	5	6	7
8	9	10	11	12	13	14
15	16	17	18	19	20	21
22	23	24	25	26	27	28
29	30					

MAY
M	T	W	T	F	S	S
	1	2	3	4	5
6	7	8	9	10	11	12
13	14	15	16	17	18	19
20	21	22	23	24	25	26
27	28	29	30	31		

JUNE
M	T	W	T	F	S	S
					1	2
3	4	5	6	7	8	9
10	11	12	13	14	15	16
17	18	19	20	21	22	23
24	25	26	27	28	29	30

JULY
M	T	W	T	F	S	S
1	2	3	4	5	6	7
8	9	10	11	12	13	14
15	16	17	18	19	20	21
22	23	24	25	26	27	28
29	30	31				

AUGUST
M	T	W	T	F	S	S
			1	2	3	4
5	6	7	8	9	10	11
12	13	14	15	16	17	18
19	20	21	22	23	24	25
26	27	28	29	30	31	

SEPTEMBER
M	T	W	T	F	S	S
						1
2	3	4	5	6	7	8
9	10	11	12	13	14	15
16	17	18	19	20	21	22
23	24	25	26	27	28	29
30						

OCTOBER
M	T	W	T	F	S	S
1	2	3	4	5	6
7	8	9	10	11	12	13
14	15	16	17	18	19	20
21	22	23	24	25	26	27
28	29	30	31			

NOVEMBER
M	T	W	T	F	S	S
				1	2	3
4	5	6	7	8	9	10
11	12	13	14	15	16	17
18	19	20	21	22	23	24
25	26	27	28	29	30	

DECEMBER
M	T	W	T	F	S	S
						1
2	3	4	5	6	7	8
9	10	11	12	13	14	15
16	17	18	19	20	21	22
23	24	25	26	27	28	29
30	31					

2025

JANUARY

M	T	W	T	F	S	S
		1	2	3	4	5
6	7	8	9	10	11	12
13	14	15	16	17	18	19
20	21	22	23	24	25	26
27	28	29	30	31		

FEBRUARY

M	T	W	T	F	S	S
					1	2
3	4	5	6	7	8	9
10	11	12	13	14	15	16
17	18	19	20	21	22	23
24	25	26	27	28		

MARCH

M	T	W	T	F	S	S
					1	2
3	4	5	6	7	8	9
10	11	12	13	14	15	16
17	18	19	20	21	22	23
24	25	26	27	28	29	30
31						

APRIL

M	T	W	T	F	S	S
	1	2	3	4	5	6
7	8	9	10	11	12	13
14	15	16	17	18	19	20
21	22	23	24	25	26	27
28	29	30				

MAY

M	T	W	T	F	S	S
			1	2	3	4
5	6	7	8	9	10	11
12	13	14	15	16	17	18
19	20	21	22	23	24	25
26	27	28	29	30	31	

JUNE

M	T	W	T	F	S	S
						1
2	3	4	5	6	7	8
9	10	11	12	13	14	15
16	17	18	19	20	21	22
23	24	25	26	27	28	29
30						

JULY

M	T	W	T	F	S	S
	1	2	3	4	5	6
7	8	9	10	11	12	13
14	15	16	17	18	19	20
21	22	23	24	25	26	27
28	29	30	31			

AUGUST

M	T	W	T	F	S	S
				1	2	3
4	5	6	7	8	9	10
11	12	13	14	15	16	17
18	19	20	21	22	23	24
25	26	27	28	29	30	31

SEPTEMBER

M	T	W	T	F	S	S
1	2	3	4	5	6	7
8	9	10	11	12	13	14
15	16	17	18	19	20	21
22	23	24	25	26	27	28
29	30					

OCTOBER

M	T	W	T	F	S	S
		1	2	3	4	5
6	7	8	9	10	11	12
13	14	15	16	17	18	19
20	21	22	23	24	25	26
27	28	29	30	31		

NOVEMBER

M	T	W	T	F	S	S
					1	2
3	4	5	6	7	8	9
10	11	12	13	14	15	16
17	18	19	20	21	22	23
24	25	26	27	28	29	30

DECEMBER

M	T	W	T	F	S	S
1	2	3	4	5	6	7
8	9	10	11	12	13	14
15	16	17	18	19	20	21
22	23	24	25	26	27	28
29	30	31				

2026

JANUARY

M	T	W	T	F	S	S
			1	2	3	4
5	6	7	8	9	10	11
12	13	14	15	16	17	18
19	20	21	22	23	24	25
26	27	28	29	30	31	

FEBRUARY

M	T	W	T	F	S	S
						1
2	3	4	5	6	7	8
9	10	11	12	13	14	15
16	17	18	19	20	21	22
23	24	25	26	27	28	

MARCH

M	T	W	T	F	S	S
						1
2	3	4	5	6	7	8
9	10	11	12	13	14	15
16	17	18	19	20	21	22
23	24	25	26	27	28	29
30	31					

APRIL

M	T	W	T	F	S	S
		1	2	3	4	5
6	7	8	9	10	11	12
13	14	15	16	17	18	19
20	21	22	23	24	25	26
27	28	29	30			

MAY

M	T	W	T	F	S	S
				1	2	3
4	5	6	7	8	9	10
11	12	13	14	15	16	17
18	19	20	21	22	23	24
25	26	27	28	29	30	31

JUNE

M	T	W	T	F	S	S
1	2	3	4	5	6	7
8	9	10	11	12	13	14
15	16	17	18	19	20	21
22	23	24	25	26	27	28
29	30					

JULY

M	T	W	T	F	S	S
		1	2	3	4	5
6	7	8	9	10	11	12
13	14	15	16	17	18	19
20	21	22	23	24	25	26
27	28	29	30	31		

AUGUST

M	T	W	T	F	S	S
					1	2
3	4	5	6	7	8	9
10	11	12	13	14	15	16
17	18	19	20	21	22	23
24	25	26	27	28	29	30
31						

SEPTEMBER

M	T	W	T	F	S	S
	1	2	3	4	5	6
7	8	9	10	11	12	13
14	15	16	17	18	19	20
21	22	23	24	25	26	27
28	29	30				

OCTOBER

M	T	W	T	F	S	S
			1	2	3	4
5	6	7	8	9	10	11
12	13	14	15	16	17	18
19	20	21	22	23	24	25
26	27	28	29	30	31	

NOVEMBER

M	T	W	T	F	S	S
						1
2	3	4	5	6	7	8
9	10	11	12	13	14	15
16	17	18	19	20	21	22
23	24	25	26	27	28	29
30						

DECEMBER

M	T	W	T	F	S	S
	1	2	3	4	5	6
7	8	9	10	11	12	13
14	15	16	17	18	19	20
21	22	23	24	25	26	27
28	29	30	31			

MONTH OF	MONDAY	TUESDAY	WEDNESDAY
WHAT WORKED LAST MONTH?	☐	☐	☐
	☐	☐	☐
WHAT COULD BE IMPROVED?	☐	☐	☐
	☐	☐	☐
THIS MONTH'S GOAL / FOCUS	☐	☐	☐
	☐	☐	☐

BIRTHDAYS THIS MONTH	OTHER IMPORTANT DATES	PLACES TO GO	PEOPLE TO SEE

THURSDAY	FRIDAY	SATURDAY	SUNDAY
☐	☐	☐	☐
☐	☐	☐	☐
☐	☐	☐	☐
☐	☐	☐	☐
☐	☐	☐	☐
☐	☐	☐	☐

HIGHLIGHTS / REFLECTION / BREAKTHROUGH

**MAXIMIZE
YOUR LIFE
PLANNER**

MONTH OF	MONDAY	TUESDAY	WEDNESDAY
WHAT WORKED LAST MONTH?	☐	☐	☐
	☐	☐	☐
WHAT COULD BE IMPROVED?	☐	☐	☐
	☐	☐	☐
THIS MONTH'S GOAL / FOCUS	☐	☐	☐
	☐	☐	☐

BIRTHDAYS THIS MONTH	OTHER IMPORTANT DATES	PLACES TO GO	PEOPLE TO SEE

THURSDAY	FRIDAY	SATURDAY	SUNDAY
☐	☐	☐	☐
☐	☐	☐	☐
☐	☐	☐	☐
☐	☐	☐	☐
☐	☐	☐	☐
☐	☐	☐	☐

HIGHLIGHTS / REFLECTION / BREAKTHROUGH

MAXIMIZE YOUR LIFE PLANNER

MONTH OF

MONDAY	TUESDAY	WEDNESDAY

BIRTHDAYS THIS MONTH

OTHER IMPORTANT DATES

PLACES TO GO

PEOPLE TO SEE

THURSDAY	FRIDAY	SATURDAY	SUNDAY
☐	☐	☐	☐
☐	☐	☐	☐
☐	☐	☐	☐
☐	☐	☐	☐
☐	☐	☐	☐
☐	☐	☐	☐

HIGHLIGHTS / REFLECTION / BREAKTHROUGH

**MAXIMIZE
YOUR LIFE
P L A N N E R**

	MONDAY	TUESDAY	WEDNESDAY
WHAT WORKED LAST MONTH?	☐	☐	☐
	☐	☐	☐
WHAT COULD BE IMPROVED?	☐	☐	☐
	☐	☐	☐
THIS MONTH'S GOAL / FOCUS	☐	☐	☐
	☐	☐	☐

BIRTHDAYS THIS MONTH

_____
_____
_____
_____
_____
_____

OTHER IMPORTANT DATES

_____
_____
_____
_____
_____
_____

PLACES TO GO

_____
_____
_____
_____
_____
_____

PEOPLE TO SEE

_____
_____
_____
_____
_____
_____

THURSDAY	FRIDAY	SATURDAY	SUNDAY
☐	☐	☐	☐
☐	☐	☐	☐
☐	☐	☐	☐
☐	☐	☐	☐
☐	☐	☐	☐
☐	☐	☐	☐

HIGHLIGHTS / REFLECTION / BREAKTHROUGH

**MAXIMIZE
YOUR LIFE
PLANNER**

MONTH OF	MONDAY	TUESDAY	WEDNESDAY
WHAT WORKED LAST MONTH?			
WHAT COULD BE IMPROVED?			
THIS MONTH'S GOAL / FOCUS			

BIRTHDAYS THIS MONTH	OTHER IMPORTANT DATES	PLACES TO GO	PEOPLE TO SEE

THURSDAY	FRIDAY	SATURDAY	SUNDAY
☐	☐	☐	☐
☐	☐	☐	☐
☐	☐	☐	☐
☐	☐	☐	☐
☐	☐	☐	☐
☐	☐	☐	☐

HIGHLIGHTS / REFLECTION / BREAKTHROUGH

**MAXIMIZE
YOUR LIFE
P L A N N E R**

MONTH OF	MONDAY	TUESDAY	WEDNESDAY
WHAT WORKED LAST MONTH?	☐	☐	☐
	☐	☐	☐
WHAT COULD BE IMPROVED?	☐	☐	☐
	☐	☐	☐
THIS MONTH'S GOAL / FOCUS	☐	☐	☐
	☐	☐	☐

BIRTHDAYS THIS MONTH	OTHER IMPORTANT DATES	PLACES TO GO	PEOPLE TO SEE
_____	_____	_____	_____
_____	_____	_____	_____
_____	_____	_____	_____
_____	_____	_____	_____
_____	_____	_____	_____
_____	_____	_____	_____

THURSDAY	FRIDAY	SATURDAY	SUNDAY
☐	☐	☐	☐
☐	☐	☐	☐
☐	☐	☐	☐
☐	☐	☐	☐
☐	☐	☐	☐
☐	☐	☐	☐

HIGHLIGHTS / REFLECTION / BREAKTHROUGH

MAXIMIZE YOUR LIFE P L A N N E R

MONTH OF

WHAT WORKED LAST MONTH?

WHAT COULD BE IMPROVED?

THIS MONTH'S GOAL / FOCUS

MONDAY	TUESDAY	WEDNESDAY
☐	☐	☐
☐	☐	☐
☐	☐	☐
☐	☐	☐
☐	☐	☐
☐	☐	☐

BIRTHDAYS THIS MONTH

OTHER IMPORTANT DATES

PLACES TO GO

PEOPLE TO SEE

THURSDAY	FRIDAY	SATURDAY	SUNDAY
☐	☐	☐	☐
☐	☐	☐	☐
☐	☐	☐	☐
☐	☐	☐	☐
☐	☐	☐	☐
☐	☐	☐	☐

HIGHLIGHTS / REFLECTION / BREAKTHROUGH

MAXIMIZE YOUR LIFE PLANNER

MONTH OF	MONDAY	TUESDAY	WEDNESDAY
WHAT WORKED LAST MONTH?	□	□	□
	□	□	□
WHAT COULD BE IMPROVED?	□	□	□
	□	□	□
THIS MONTH'S GOAL / FOCUS	□	□	□
	□	□	□

BIRTHDAYS THIS MONTH	OTHER IMPORTANT DATES	PLACES TO GO	PEOPLE TO SEE
_____	_____	_____	_____
_____	_____	_____	_____
_____	_____	_____	_____
_____	_____	_____	_____
_____	_____	_____	_____
_____	_____	_____	_____

THURSDAY	FRIDAY	SATURDAY	SUNDAY
☐	☐	☐	☐
☐	☐	☐	☐
☐	☐	☐	☐
☐	☐	☐	☐
☐	☐	☐	☐
☐	☐	☐	☐

HIGHLIGHTS / REFLECTION / BREAKTHROUGH

**MAXIMIZE
YOUR LIFE
PLANNER**

MONTH OF	MONDAY	TUESDAY	WEDNESDAY
WHAT WORKED LAST MONTH?	☐	☐	☐
	☐	☐	☐
WHAT COULD BE IMPROVED?	☐	☐	☐
	☐	☐	☐
THIS MONTH'S GOAL / FOCUS	☐	☐	☐
	☐	☐	☐

BIRTHDAYS THIS MONTH	OTHER IMPORTANT DATES	PLACES TO GO	PEOPLE TO SEE
_____	_____	_____	_____
_____	_____	_____	_____
_____	_____	_____	_____
_____	_____	_____	_____
_____	_____	_____	_____
_____	_____	_____	_____

THURSDAY	FRIDAY	SATURDAY	SUNDAY
☐	☐	☐	☐
☐	☐	☐	☐
☐	☐	☐	☐
☐	☐	☐	☐
☐	☐	☐	☐
☐	☐	☐	☐

HIGHLIGHTS / REFLECTION / BREAKTHROUGH

_____

_____

_____

_____

_____

_____

**MAXIMIZE
YOUR LIFE
P L A N N E R**

MONTH OF	MONDAY	TUESDAY	WEDNESDAY
WHAT WORKED LAST MONTH?	☐	☐	☐
	☐	☐	☐
WHAT COULD BE IMPROVED?	☐	☐	☐
	☐	☐	☐
THIS MONTH'S GOAL / FOCUS	☐	☐	☐
	☐	☐	☐

BIRTHDAYS THIS MONTH	OTHER IMPORTANT DATES	PLACES TO GO	PEOPLE TO SEE
_____	_____	_____	_____
_____	_____	_____	_____
_____	_____	_____	_____
_____	_____	_____	_____
_____	_____	_____	_____
_____	_____	_____	_____
_____	_____	_____	_____

THURSDAY	FRIDAY	SATURDAY	SUNDAY
☐	☐	☐	☐
☐	☐	☐	☐
☐	☐	☐	☐
☐	☐	☐	☐
☐	☐	☐	☐
☐	☐	☐	☐

HIGHLIGHTS / REFLECTION / BREAKTHROUGH

**MAXIMIZE
YOUR LIFE
P L A N N E R**

	MONDAY	TUESDAY	WEDNESDAY
MONTH OF	☐	☐	☐
WHAT WORKED LAST MONTH?			
	☐	☐	☐
WHAT COULD BE IMPROVED?	☐	☐	☐
	☐	☐	☐
THIS MONTH'S GOAL / FOCUS	☐	☐	☐
	☐	☐	☐

BIRTHDAYS THIS MONTH

_____
_____
_____
_____
_____
_____

OTHER IMPORTANT DATES

_____
_____
_____
_____
_____
_____

PLACES TO GO

_____
_____
_____
_____
_____
_____

PEOPLE TO SEE

_____
_____
_____
_____
_____
_____

THURSDAY	FRIDAY	SATURDAY	SUNDAY
☐	☐	☐	☐
☐	☐	☐	☐
☐	☐	☐	☐
☐	☐	☐	☐
☐	☐	☐	☐
☐	☐	☐	☐

HIGHLIGHTS / REFLECTION / BREAKTHROUGH

MAXIMIZE YOUR LIFE PLANNER

	MONDAY	TUESDAY	WEDNESDAY
MONTH OF	☐	☐	☐
WHAT WORKED LAST MONTH?	☐	☐	☐
	☐	☐	☐
WHAT COULD BE IMPROVED?	☐	☐	☐
THIS MONTH'S GOAL / FOCUS	☐	☐	☐
	☐	☐	☐

BIRTHDAYS THIS MONTH	OTHER IMPORTANT DATES	PLACES TO GO	PEOPLE TO SEE
_____	_____	_____	_____
_____	_____	_____	_____
_____	_____	_____	_____
_____	_____	_____	_____
_____	_____	_____	_____
_____	_____	_____	_____

THURSDAY	FRIDAY	SATURDAY	SUNDAY
☐	☐	☐	☐
☐	☐	☐	☐
☐	☐	☐	☐
☐	☐	☐	☐
☐	☐	☐	☐
☐	☐	☐	☐

HIGHLIGHTS / REFLECTION / BREAKTHROUGH

MAXIMIZE YOUR LIFE PLANNER

10 BEFORE 10 GRATITUDE LIST

Take note of 10 things you're grateful for before 10am

Date: _____

1. _____   6. _____
2. _____   7. _____
3. _____   8. _____
4. _____   9. _____
5. _____   10. _____

Date: _____

1. _____   6. _____
2. _____   7. _____
3. _____   8. _____
4. _____   9. _____
5. _____   10. _____

Date: _____

1. _____   6. _____
2. _____   7. _____
3. _____   8. _____
4. _____   9. _____
5. _____   10. _____

Date: _____

1. _____   6. _____
2. _____   7. _____
3. _____   8. _____
4. _____   9. _____
5. _____   10. _____

Date: _____

1. _____   6. _____
2. _____   7. _____
3. _____   8. _____
4. _____   9. _____
5. _____   10. _____

Date: _____

1. _____   6. _____
2. _____   7. _____
3. _____   8. _____
4. _____   9. _____
5. _____   10. _____

Date: _____

1. _____   6. _____
2. _____   7. _____
3. _____   8. _____
4. _____   9. _____
5. _____   10. _____

Date: _____

1. _____   6. _____
2. _____   7. _____
3. _____   8. _____
4. _____   9. _____
5. _____   10. _____

Date: _____

1. _____   6. _____
2. _____   7. _____
3. _____   8. _____
4. _____   9. _____
5. _____   10. _____

Date: _____

1. _____   6. _____
2. _____   7. _____
3. _____   8. _____
4. _____   9. _____
5. _____   10. _____

Date: _____

1. _____   6. _____
2. _____   7. _____
3. _____   8. _____
4. _____   9. _____
5. _____   10. _____

Date: _____

1. _____   6. _____
2. _____   7. _____
3. _____   8. _____
4. _____   9. _____
5. _____   10. _____

Date: _____

1. _____   6. _____
2. _____   7. _____
3. _____   8. _____
4. _____   9. _____
5. _____   10. _____

Date: _____

1. _____   6. _____
2. _____   7. _____
3. _____   8. _____
4. _____   9. _____
5. _____   10. _____

10 *BEFORE* 10 **GRATITUDE** LIST

Date: _____

1. _____   6. _____
2. _____   7. _____
3. _____   8. _____
4. _____   9. _____
5. _____   10. _____

Date: _____

1. _____   6. _____
2. _____   7. _____
3. _____   8. _____
4. _____   9. _____
5. _____   10. _____

Date: _____

1. _____   6. _____
2. _____   7. _____
3. _____   8. _____
4. _____   9. _____
5. _____   10. _____

Date: _____

1. _____   6. _____
2. _____   7. _____
3. _____   8. _____
4. _____   9. _____
5. _____   10. _____

Date: _____

1. _____   6. _____
2. _____   7. _____
3. _____   8. _____
4. _____   9. _____
5. _____   10. _____

Date: _____

1. _____   6. _____
2. _____   7. _____
3. _____   8. _____
4. _____   9. _____
5. _____   10. _____

Date: _____

1. _____   6. _____
2. _____   7. _____
3. _____   8. _____
4. _____   9. _____
5. _____   10. _____

Date: _____

1. _____   6. _____
2. _____   7. _____
3. _____   8. _____
4. _____   9. _____
5. _____   10. _____

Date: _____

1. _____   6. _____
2. _____   7. _____
3. _____   8. _____
4. _____   9. _____
5. _____   10. _____

Date: _____

1. _____   6. _____
2. _____   7. _____
3. _____   8. _____
4. _____   9. _____
5. _____   10. _____

Date: _____

1. _____   6. _____
2. _____   7. _____
3. _____   8. _____
4. _____   9. _____
5. _____   10. _____

Date: _____

1. _____   6. _____
2. _____   7. _____
3. _____   8. _____
4. _____   9. _____
5. _____   10. _____

Date: _____

1. _____   6. _____
2. _____   7. _____
3. _____   8. _____
4. _____   9. _____
5. _____   10. _____

Date: _____

1. _____   6. _____
2. _____   7. _____
3. _____   8. _____
4. _____   9. _____
5. _____   10. _____

10 *BEFORE* 10 **GRATITUDE** LIST

Take note of 10 things you're grateful for before 10am

Date: _____

1. _____   6. _____
2. _____   7. _____
3. _____   8. _____
4. _____   9. _____
5. _____   10. _____

Date: _____

1. _____   6. _____
2. _____   7. _____
3. _____   8. _____
4. _____   9. _____
5. _____   10. _____

Date: _____

1. _____   6. _____
2. _____   7. _____
3. _____   8. _____
4. _____   9. _____
5. _____   10. _____

Date: _____

1. _____   6. _____
2. _____   7. _____
3. _____   8. _____
4. _____   9. _____
5. _____   10. _____

Date: _____

1. _____   6. _____
2. _____   7. _____
3. _____   8. _____
4. _____   9. _____
5. _____   10. _____

Date: _____

1. _____   6. _____
2. _____   7. _____
3. _____   8. _____
4. _____   9. _____
5. _____   10. _____

Date: _____

1. _____   6. _____
2. _____   7. _____
3. _____   8. _____
4. _____   9. _____
5. _____   10. _____

Date: _____

1. _____   6. _____
2. _____   7. _____
3. _____   8. _____
4. _____   9. _____
5. _____   10. _____

Date: _____

1. _____   6. _____
2. _____   7. _____
3. _____   8. _____
4. _____   9. _____
5. _____   10. _____

Date: _____

1. _____   6. _____
2. _____   7. _____
3. _____   8. _____
4. _____   9. _____
5. _____   10. _____

Date: _____

1. _____   6. _____
2. _____   7. _____
3. _____   8. _____
4. _____   9. _____
5. _____   10. _____

Date: _____

1. _____   6. _____
2. _____   7. _____
3. _____   8. _____
4. _____   9. _____
5. _____   10. _____

10 BEFORE 10 GRATITUDE LIST

Take note of 10 things you're grateful for before 10am

Date: _____

1. _____   6. _____
2. _____   7. _____
3. _____   8. _____
4. _____   9. _____
5. _____   10. _____

Date: _____

1. _____   6. _____
2. _____   7. _____
3. _____   8. _____
4. _____   9. _____
5. _____   10. _____

Date: _____

1. _____   6. _____
2. _____   7. _____
3. _____   8. _____
4. _____   9. _____
5. _____   10. _____

Date: _____

1. _____   6. _____
2. _____   7. _____
3. _____   8. _____
4. _____   9. _____
5. _____   10. _____

Date: _____

1. _____   6. _____
2. _____   7. _____
3. _____   8. _____
4. _____   9. _____
5. _____   10. _____

Date: _____

1. _____   6. _____
2. _____   7. _____
3. _____   8. _____
4. _____   9. _____
5. _____   10. _____

Date: _____

1. _____   6. _____
2. _____   7. _____
3. _____   8. _____
4. _____   9. _____
5. _____   10. _____

Date: _____

1. _____   6. _____
2. _____   7. _____
3. _____   8. _____
4. _____   9. _____
5. _____   10. _____

Date: _____

1. _____   6. _____
2. _____   7. _____
3. _____   8. _____
4. _____   9. _____
5. _____   10. _____

Date: _____

1. _____   6. _____
2. _____   7. _____
3. _____   8. _____
4. _____   9. _____
5. _____   10. _____

Date: _____

1. _____   6. _____
2. _____   7. _____
3. _____   8. _____
4. _____   9. _____
5. _____   10. _____

Date: _____

1. _____   6. _____
2. _____   7. _____
3. _____   8. _____
4. _____   9. _____
5. _____   10. _____

10 *BEFORE* 10 **GRATITUDE** LIST

Date: _____

1. _____ 6. _____
2. _____ 7. _____
3. _____ 8. _____
4. _____ 9. _____
5. _____ 10. _____

Date: _____

1. _____ 6. _____
2. _____ 7. _____
3. _____ 8. _____
4. _____ 9. _____
5. _____ 10. _____

Date: _____

1. _____ 6. _____
2. _____ 7. _____
3. _____ 8. _____
4. _____ 9. _____
5. _____ 10. _____

Date: _____

1. _____ 6. _____
2. _____ 7. _____
3. _____ 8. _____
4. _____ 9. _____
5. _____ 10. _____

Date: _____

1. _____ 6. _____
2. _____ 7. _____
3. _____ 8. _____
4. _____ 9. _____
5. _____ 10. _____

Date: _____

1. _____ 6. _____
2. _____ 7. _____
3. _____ 8. _____
4. _____ 9. _____
5. _____ 10. _____

Date: _____

1. _____ 6. _____
2. _____ 7. _____
3. _____ 8. _____
4. _____ 9. _____
5. _____ 10. _____

Date: _____

1. _____ 6. _____
2. _____ 7. _____
3. _____ 8. _____
4. _____ 9. _____
5. _____ 10. _____

Date: _____

1. _____ 6. _____
2. _____ 7. _____
3. _____ 8. _____
4. _____ 9. _____
5. _____ 10. _____

Date: _____

1. _____ 6. _____
2. _____ 7. _____
3. _____ 8. _____
4. _____ 9. _____
5. _____ 10. _____

Date: _____

1. _____ 6. _____
2. _____ 7. _____
3. _____ 8. _____
4. _____ 9. _____
5. _____ 10. _____

Date: _____

1. _____ 6. _____
2. _____ 7. _____
3. _____ 8. _____
4. _____ 9. _____
5. _____ 10. _____

Date: _____

1. _____ 6. _____
2. _____ 7. _____
3. _____ 8. _____
4. _____ 9. _____
5. _____ 10. _____

Date: _____

1. _____ 6. _____
2. _____ 7. _____
3. _____ 8. _____
4. _____ 9. _____
5. _____ 10. _____

10 *BEFORE* 10 **GRATITUDE** LIST

Take note of 10 things you're grateful for before 10am

Date: _____

1. _____
2. _____
3. _____
4. _____
5. _____
6. _____
7. _____
8. _____
9. _____
10. _____

Date: _____

1. _____
2. _____
3. _____
4. _____
5. _____
6. _____
7. _____
8. _____
9. _____
10. _____

Date: _____

1. _____
2. _____
3. _____
4. _____
5. _____
6. _____
7. _____
8. _____
9. _____
10. _____

Date: _____

1. _____
2. _____
3. _____
4. _____
5. _____
6. _____
7. _____
8. _____
9. _____
10. _____

Date: _____

1. _____
2. _____
3. _____
4. _____
5. _____
6. _____
7. _____
8. _____
9. _____
10. _____

Date: _____

1. _____
2. _____
3. _____
4. _____
5. _____
6. _____
7. _____
8. _____
9. _____
10. _____

Date: _____

1. _____
2. _____
3. _____
4. _____
5. _____
6. _____
7. _____
8. _____
9. _____
10. _____

Date: _____

1. _____
2. _____
3. _____
4. _____
5. _____
6. _____
7. _____
8. _____
9. _____
10. _____

Date: _____

1. _____
2. _____
3. _____
4. _____
5. _____
6. _____
7. _____
8. _____
9. _____
10. _____

Date: _____

1. _____
2. _____
3. _____
4. _____
5. _____
6. _____
7. _____
8. _____
9. _____
10. _____

Date: _____

1. _____
2. _____
3. _____
4. _____
5. _____
6. _____
7. _____
8. _____
9. _____
10. _____

Date: _____

1. _____
2. _____
3. _____
4. _____
5. _____
6. _____
7. _____
8. _____
9. _____
10. _____

Date: _____

1. _____
2. _____
3. _____
4. _____
5. _____
6. _____
7. _____
8. _____
9. _____
10. _____

Date: _____

1. _____
2. _____
3. _____
4. _____
5. _____
6. _____
7. _____
8. _____
9. _____
10. _____

10 *BEFORE* 10 **GRATITUDE** LIST

Take note of 10 things you're grateful for before 10am

Date: _____

1. _____ 6. _____
2. _____ 7. _____
3. _____ 8. _____
4. _____ 9. _____
5. _____ 10. _____

Date: _____

1. _____ 6. _____
2. _____ 7. _____
3. _____ 8. _____
4. _____ 9. _____
5. _____ 10. _____

Date: _____

1. _____ 6. _____
2. _____ 7. _____
3. _____ 8. _____
4. _____ 9. _____
5. _____ 10. _____

Date: _____

1. _____ 6. _____
2. _____ 7. _____
3. _____ 8. _____
4. _____ 9. _____
5. _____ 10. _____

Date: _____

1. _____ 6. _____
2. _____ 7. _____
3. _____ 8. _____
4. _____ 9. _____
5. _____ 10. _____

Date: _____

1. _____ 6. _____
2. _____ 7. _____
3. _____ 8. _____
4. _____ 9. _____
5. _____ 10. _____

Date: _____

1. _____ 6. _____
2. _____ 7. _____
3. _____ 8. _____
4. _____ 9. _____
5. _____ 10. _____

Date: _____

1. _____ 6. _____
2. _____ 7. _____
3. _____ 8. _____
4. _____ 9. _____
5. _____ 10. _____

Date: _____

1. _____ 6. _____
2. _____ 7. _____
3. _____ 8. _____
4. _____ 9. _____
5. _____ 10. _____

Date: _____

1. _____ 6. _____
2. _____ 7. _____
3. _____ 8. _____
4. _____ 9. _____
5. _____ 10. _____

Date: _____

1. _____ 6. _____
2. _____ 7. _____
3. _____ 8. _____
4. _____ 9. _____
5. _____ 10. _____

Date: _____

1. _____ 6. _____
2. _____ 7. _____
3. _____ 8. _____
4. _____ 9. _____
5. _____ 10. _____

10 *BEFORE* 10 **GRATITUDE** LIST

Take note of 10 things you're grateful for before 10am

Date: _____

1. _____   6. _____
2. _____   7. _____
3. _____   8. _____
4. _____   9. _____
5. _____   10. _____

Date: _____

1. _____   6. _____
2. _____   7. _____
3. _____   8. _____
4. _____   9. _____
5. _____   10. _____

Date: _____

1. _____   6. _____
2. _____   7. _____
3. _____   8. _____
4. _____   9. _____
5. _____   10. _____

Date: _____

1. _____   6. _____
2. _____   7. _____
3. _____   8. _____
4. _____   9. _____
5. _____   10. _____

Date: _____

1. _____   6. _____
2. _____   7. _____
3. _____   8. _____
4. _____   9. _____
5. _____   10. _____

Date: _____

1. _____   6. _____
2. _____   7. _____
3. _____   8. _____
4. _____   9. _____
5. _____   10. _____

Date: _____

1. _____   6. _____
2. _____   7. _____
3. _____   8. _____
4. _____   9. _____
5. _____   10. _____

Date: _____

1. _____   6. _____
2. _____   7. _____
3. _____   8. _____
4. _____   9. _____
5. _____   10. _____

Date: _____

1. _____   6. _____
2. _____   7. _____
3. _____   8. _____
4. _____   9. _____
5. _____   10. _____

Date: _____

1. _____   6. _____
2. _____   7. _____
3. _____   8. _____
4. _____   9. _____
5. _____   10. _____

Date: _____

1. _____   6. _____
2. _____   7. _____
3. _____   8. _____
4. _____   9. _____
5. _____   10. _____

Date: _____

1. _____   6. _____
2. _____   7. _____
3. _____   8. _____
4. _____   9. _____
5. _____   10. _____

10 *BEFORE* 10 **GRATITUDE** LIST

Take note of 10 things you're grateful for before 10am

Date: _____

1. _____ 6. _____
2. _____ 7. _____
3. _____ 8. _____
4. _____ 9. _____
5. _____ 10. _____

Date: _____

1. _____ 6. _____
2. _____ 7. _____
3. _____ 8. _____
4. _____ 9. _____
5. _____ 10. _____

Date: _____

1. _____ 6. _____
2. _____ 7. _____
3. _____ 8. _____
4. _____ 9. _____
5. _____ 10. _____

Date: _____

1. _____ 6. _____
2. _____ 7. _____
3. _____ 8. _____
4. _____ 9. _____
5. _____ 10. _____

Date: _____

1. _____ 6. _____
2. _____ 7. _____
3. _____ 8. _____
4. _____ 9. _____
5. _____ 10. _____

Date: _____

1. _____ 6. _____
2. _____ 7. _____
3. _____ 8. _____
4. _____ 9. _____
5. _____ 10. _____

Date: _____

1. _____ 6. _____
2. _____ 7. _____
3. _____ 8. _____
4. _____ 9. _____
5. _____ 10. _____

Date: _____

1. _____ 6. _____
2. _____ 7. _____
3. _____ 8. _____
4. _____ 9. _____
5. _____ 10. _____

Date: _____

1. _____ 6. _____
2. _____ 7. _____
3. _____ 8. _____
4. _____ 9. _____
5. _____ 10. _____

Date: _____

1. _____ 6. _____
2. _____ 7. _____
3. _____ 8. _____
4. _____ 9. _____
5. _____ 10. _____

Date: _____

1. _____ 6. _____
2. _____ 7. _____
3. _____ 8. _____
4. _____ 9. _____
5. _____ 10. _____

Date: _____

1. _____ 6. _____
2. _____ 7. _____
3. _____ 8. _____
4. _____ 9. _____
5. _____ 10. _____

10 *BEFORE* 10 **GRATITUDE** LIST

Take note of 10 things you're grateful for before 10am

Date: _____

1. _____
2. _____
3. _____
4. _____
5. _____
6. _____
7. _____
8. _____
9. _____
10. _____

Date: _____

1. _____
2. _____
3. _____
4. _____
5. _____
6. _____
7. _____
8. _____
9. _____
10. _____

Date: _____

1. _____
2. _____
3. _____
4. _____
5. _____
6. _____
7. _____
8. _____
9. _____
10. _____

Date: _____

1. _____
2. _____
3. _____
4. _____
5. _____
6. _____
7. _____
8. _____
9. _____
10. _____

Date: _____

1. _____
2. _____
3. _____
4. _____
5. _____
6. _____
7. _____
8. _____
9. _____
10. _____

Date: _____

1. _____
2. _____
3. _____
4. _____
5. _____
6. _____
7. _____
8. _____
9. _____
10. _____

Date: _____

1. _____
2. _____
3. _____
4. _____
5. _____
6. _____
7. _____
8. _____
9. _____
10. _____

Date: _____

1. _____
2. _____
3. _____
4. _____
5. _____
6. _____
7. _____
8. _____
9. _____
10. _____

Date: _____

1. _____
2. _____
3. _____
4. _____
5. _____
6. _____
7. _____
8. _____
9. _____
10. _____

Date: _____

1. _____
2. _____
3. _____
4. _____
5. _____
6. _____
7. _____
8. _____
9. _____
10. _____

Date: _____

1. _____
2. _____
3. _____
4. _____
5. _____
6. _____
7. _____
8. _____
9. _____
10. _____

Date: _____

1. _____
2. _____
3. _____
4. _____
5. _____
6. _____
7. _____
8. _____
9. _____
10. _____

Date: _____

1. _____
2. _____
3. _____
4. _____
5. _____
6. _____
7. _____
8. _____
9. _____
10. _____

Date: _____

1. _____
2. _____
3. _____
4. _____
5. _____
6. _____
7. _____
8. _____
9. _____
10. _____

10 *BEFORE* **10 GRATITUDE** LIST

Date: _____

1. _____ 6. _____
2. _____ 7. _____
3. _____ 8. _____
4. _____ 9. _____
5. _____ 10. _____

Date: _____

1. _____ 6. _____
2. _____ 7. _____
3. _____ 8. _____
4. _____ 9. _____
5. _____ 10. _____

Date: _____

1. _____ 6. _____
2. _____ 7. _____
3. _____ 8. _____
4. _____ 9. _____
5. _____ 10. _____

Date: _____

1. _____ 6. _____
2. _____ 7. _____
3. _____ 8. _____
4. _____ 9. _____
5. _____ 10. _____

Date: _____

1. _____ 6. _____
2. _____ 7. _____
3. _____ 8. _____
4. _____ 9. _____
5. _____ 10. _____

Date: _____

1. _____ 6. _____
2. _____ 7. _____
3. _____ 8. _____
4. _____ 9. _____
5. _____ 10. _____

Date: _____

1. _____ 6. _____
2. _____ 7. _____
3. _____ 8. _____
4. _____ 9. _____
5. _____ 10. _____

Date: _____

1. _____ 6. _____
2. _____ 7. _____
3. _____ 8. _____
4. _____ 9. _____
5. _____ 10. _____

Date: _____

1. _____ 6. _____
2. _____ 7. _____
3. _____ 8. _____
4. _____ 9. _____
5. _____ 10. _____

Date: _____

1. _____ 6. _____
2. _____ 7. _____
3. _____ 8. _____
4. _____ 9. _____
5. _____ 10. _____

Date: _____

1. _____ 6. _____
2. _____ 7. _____
3. _____ 8. _____
4. _____ 9. _____
5. _____ 10. _____

Date: _____

1. _____ 6. _____
2. _____ 7. _____
3. _____ 8. _____
4. _____ 9. _____
5. _____ 10. _____

10 BEFORE 10 GRATITUDE LIST

Take note of 10 things you're grateful for before 10am

Date: _____

1. _____
2. _____
3. _____
4. _____
5. _____
6. _____
7. _____
8. _____
9. _____
10. _____

Date: _____

1. _____
2. _____
3. _____
4. _____
5. _____
6. _____
7. _____
8. _____
9. _____
10. _____

Date: _____

1. _____
2. _____
3. _____
4. _____
5. _____
6. _____
7. _____
8. _____
9. _____
10. _____

Date: _____

1. _____
2. _____
3. _____
4. _____
5. _____
6. _____
7. _____
8. _____
9. _____
10. _____

Date: _____

1. _____
2. _____
3. _____
4. _____
5. _____
6. _____
7. _____
8. _____
9. _____
10. _____

Date: _____

1. _____
2. _____
3. _____
4. _____
5. _____
6. _____
7. _____
8. _____
9. _____
10. _____

Date: _____

1. _____
2. _____
3. _____
4. _____
5. _____
6. _____
7. _____
8. _____
9. _____
10. _____

Date: _____

1. _____
2. _____
3. _____
4. _____
5. _____
6. _____
7. _____
8. _____
9. _____
10. _____

Date: _____

1. _____
2. _____
3. _____
4. _____
5. _____
6. _____
7. _____
8. _____
9. _____
10. _____

Date: _____

1. _____
2. _____
3. _____
4. _____
5. _____
6. _____
7. _____
8. _____
9. _____
10. _____

Date: _____

1. _____
2. _____
3. _____
4. _____
5. _____
6. _____
7. _____
8. _____
9. _____
10. _____

Date: _____

1. _____
2. _____
3. _____
4. _____
5. _____
6. _____
7. _____
8. _____
9. _____
10. _____

Date: _____

1. _____
2. _____
3. _____
4. _____
5. _____
6. _____
7. _____
8. _____
9. _____
10. _____

Date: _____

1. _____
2. _____
3. _____
4. _____
5. _____
6. _____
7. _____
8. _____
9. _____
10. _____

10 *BEFORE* 10 **GRATITUDE** LIST

Date: _____

1. _____   6. _____
2. _____   7. _____
3. _____   8. _____
4. _____   9. _____
5. _____   10. _____

Date: _____

1. _____   6. _____
2. _____   7. _____
3. _____   8. _____
4. _____   9. _____
5. _____   10. _____

Date: _____

1. _____   6. _____
2. _____   7. _____
3. _____   8. _____
4. _____   9. _____
5. _____   10. _____

Date: _____

1. _____   6. _____
2. _____   7. _____
3. _____   8. _____
4. _____   9. _____
5. _____   10. _____

Date: _____

1. _____   6. _____
2. _____   7. _____
3. _____   8. _____
4. _____   9. _____
5. _____   10. _____

Date: _____

1. _____   6. _____
2. _____   7. _____
3. _____   8. _____
4. _____   9. _____
5. _____   10. _____

Date: _____

1. _____   6. _____
2. _____   7. _____
3. _____   8. _____
4. _____   9. _____
5. _____   10. _____

Date: _____

1. _____   6. _____
2. _____   7. _____
3. _____   8. _____
4. _____   9. _____
5. _____   10. _____

Date: _____

1. _____   6. _____
2. _____   7. _____
3. _____   8. _____
4. _____   9. _____
5. _____   10. _____

Date: _____

1. _____   6. _____
2. _____   7. _____
3. _____   8. _____
4. _____   9. _____
5. _____   10. _____

Date: _____

1. _____   6. _____
2. _____   7. _____
3. _____   8. _____
4. _____   9. _____
5. _____   10. _____

Date: _____

1. _____   6. _____
2. _____   7. _____
3. _____   8. _____
4. _____   9. _____
5. _____   10. _____

10 *BEFORE* 10 **GRATITUDE** LIST

Take note of 10 things you're grateful for before 10am

Date: _____

1. _____   6. _____
2. _____   7. _____
3. _____   8. _____
4. _____   9. _____
5. _____   10. _____

Date: _____

1. _____   6. _____
2. _____   7. _____
3. _____   8. _____
4. _____   9. _____
5. _____   10. _____

Date: _____

1. _____   6. _____
2. _____   7. _____
3. _____   8. _____
4. _____   9. _____
5. _____   10. _____

Date: _____

1. _____   6. _____
2. _____   7. _____
3. _____   8. _____
4. _____   9. _____
5. _____   10. _____

Date: _____

1. _____   6. _____
2. _____   7. _____
3. _____   8. _____
4. _____   9. _____
5. _____   10. _____

Date: _____

1. _____   6. _____
2. _____   7. _____
3. _____   8. _____
4. _____   9. _____
5. _____   10. _____

Date: _____

1. _____   6. _____
2. _____   7. _____
3. _____   8. _____
4. _____   9. _____
5. _____   10. _____

Date: _____

1. _____   6. _____
2. _____   7. _____
3. _____   8. _____
4. _____   9. _____
5. _____   10. _____

Date: _____

1. _____   6. _____
2. _____   7. _____
3. _____   8. _____
4. _____   9. _____
5. _____   10. _____

Date: _____

1. _____   6. _____
2. _____   7. _____
3. _____   8. _____
4. _____   9. _____
5. _____   10. _____

Date: _____

1. _____   6. _____
2. _____   7. _____
3. _____   8. _____
4. _____   9. _____
5. _____   10. _____

Date: _____

1. _____   6. _____
2. _____   7. _____
3. _____   8. _____
4. _____   9. _____
5. _____   10. _____

Date: _____

1. _____   6. _____
2. _____   7. _____
3. _____   8. _____
4. _____   9. _____
5. _____   10. _____

Date: _____

1. _____   6. _____
2. _____   7. _____
3. _____   8. _____
4. _____   9. _____
5. _____   10. _____

10 *BEFORE* 10 **GRATITUDE** LIST

Take note of 10 things you're grateful for before 10am

Date: _____

1. _____
2. _____
3. _____
4. _____
5. _____
6. _____
7. _____
8. _____
9. _____
10. _____

Date: _____

1. _____
2. _____
3. _____
4. _____
5. _____
6. _____
7. _____
8. _____
9. _____
10. _____

Date: _____

1. _____
2. _____
3. _____
4. _____
5. _____
6. _____
7. _____
8. _____
9. _____
10. _____

Date: _____

1. _____
2. _____
3. _____
4. _____
5. _____
6. _____
7. _____
8. _____
9. _____
10. _____

Date: _____

1. _____
2. _____
3. _____
4. _____
5. _____
6. _____
7. _____
8. _____
9. _____
10. _____

Date: _____

1. _____
2. _____
3. _____
4. _____
5. _____
6. _____
7. _____
8. _____
9. _____
10. _____

Date: _____

1. _____
2. _____
3. _____
4. _____
5. _____
6. _____
7. _____
8. _____
9. _____
10. _____

Date: _____

1. _____
2. _____
3. _____
4. _____
5. _____
6. _____
7. _____
8. _____
9. _____
10. _____

Date: _____

1. _____
2. _____
3. _____
4. _____
5. _____
6. _____
7. _____
8. _____
9. _____
10. _____

Date: _____

1. _____
2. _____
3. _____
4. _____
5. _____
6. _____
7. _____
8. _____
9. _____
10. _____

Date: _____

1. _____
2. _____
3. _____
4. _____
5. _____
6. _____
7. _____
8. _____
9. _____
10. _____

Date: _____

1. _____
2. _____
3. _____
4. _____
5. _____
6. _____
7. _____
8. _____
9. _____
10. _____

10 *BEFORE* 10 **GRATITUDE** LIST

Take note of 10 things you're grateful for before 10am

Date: _____

1. _____   6. _____
2. _____   7. _____
3. _____   8. _____
4. _____   9. _____
5. _____   10. _____

Date: _____

1. _____   6. _____
2. _____   7. _____
3. _____   8. _____
4. _____   9. _____
5. _____   10. _____

Date: _____

1. _____   6. _____
2. _____   7. _____
3. _____   8. _____
4. _____   9. _____
5. _____   10. _____

Date: _____

1. _____   6. _____
2. _____   7. _____
3. _____   8. _____
4. _____   9. _____
5. _____   10. _____

Date: _____

1. _____   6. _____
2. _____   7. _____
3. _____   8. _____
4. _____   9. _____
5. _____   10. _____

Date: _____

1. _____   6. _____
2. _____   7. _____
3. _____   8. _____
4. _____   9. _____
5. _____   10. _____

Date: _____

1. _____   6. _____
2. _____   7. _____
3. _____   8. _____
4. _____   9. _____
5. _____   10. _____

Date: _____

1. _____   6. _____
2. _____   7. _____
3. _____   8. _____
4. _____   9. _____
5. _____   10. _____

Date: _____

1. _____   6. _____
2. _____   7. _____
3. _____   8. _____
4. _____   9. _____
5. _____   10. _____

Date: _____

1. _____   6. _____
2. _____   7. _____
3. _____   8. _____
4. _____   9. _____
5. _____   10. _____

Date: _____

1. _____   6. _____
2. _____   7. _____
3. _____   8. _____
4. _____   9. _____
5. _____   10. _____

Date: _____

1. _____   6. _____
2. _____   7. _____
3. _____   8. _____
4. _____   9. _____
5. _____   10. _____

Date: _____

1. _____   6. _____
2. _____   7. _____
3. _____   8. _____
4. _____   9. _____
5. _____   10. _____

Date: _____

1. _____   6. _____
2. _____   7. _____
3. _____   8. _____
4. _____   9. _____
5. _____   10. _____

10 *BEFORE* 10 **GRATITUDE** LIST

Take note of 10 things you're grateful for before 10am

Date: _____

1. _____ 6. _____
2. _____ 7. _____
3. _____ 8. _____
4. _____ 9. _____
5. _____ 10. _____

Date: _____

1. _____ 6. _____
2. _____ 7. _____
3. _____ 8. _____
4. _____ 9. _____
5. _____ 10. _____

Date: _____

1. _____ 6. _____
2. _____ 7. _____
3. _____ 8. _____
4. _____ 9. _____
5. _____ 10. _____

Date: _____

1. _____ 6. _____
2. _____ 7. _____
3. _____ 8. _____
4. _____ 9. _____
5. _____ 10. _____

Date: _____

1. _____ 6. _____
2. _____ 7. _____
3. _____ 8. _____
4. _____ 9. _____
5. _____ 10. _____

Date: _____

1. _____ 6. _____
2. _____ 7. _____
3. _____ 8. _____
4. _____ 9. _____
5. _____ 10. _____

Date: _____

1. _____ 6. _____
2. _____ 7. _____
3. _____ 8. _____
4. _____ 9. _____
5. _____ 10. _____

Date: _____

1. _____ 6. _____
2. _____ 7. _____
3. _____ 8. _____
4. _____ 9. _____
5. _____ 10. _____

Date: _____

1. _____ 6. _____
2. _____ 7. _____
3. _____ 8. _____
4. _____ 9. _____
5. _____ 10. _____

Date: _____

1. _____ 6. _____
2. _____ 7. _____
3. _____ 8. _____
4. _____ 9. _____
5. _____ 10. _____

Date: _____

1. _____ 6. _____
2. _____ 7. _____
3. _____ 8. _____
4. _____ 9. _____
5. _____ 10. _____

Date: _____

1. _____ 6. _____
2. _____ 7. _____
3. _____ 8. _____
4. _____ 9. _____
5. _____ 10. _____

10 *BEFORE* 10 **GRATITUDE** LIST

Take note of 10 things you're grateful for before 10am

Date: _____

1. _____
2. _____
3. _____
4. _____
5. _____
6. _____
7. _____
8. _____
9. _____
10. _____

Date: _____

1. _____
2. _____
3. _____
4. _____
5. _____
6. _____
7. _____
8. _____
9. _____
10. _____

Date: _____

1. _____
2. _____
3. _____
4. _____
5. _____
6. _____
7. _____
8. _____
9. _____
10. _____

Date: _____

1. _____
2. _____
3. _____
4. _____
5. _____
6. _____
7. _____
8. _____
9. _____
10. _____

Date: _____

1. _____
2. _____
3. _____
4. _____
5. _____
6. _____
7. _____
8. _____
9. _____
10. _____

Date: _____

1. _____
2. _____
3. _____
4. _____
5. _____
6. _____
7. _____
8. _____
9. _____
10. _____

Date: _____

1. _____
2. _____
3. _____
4. _____
5. _____
6. _____
7. _____
8. _____
9. _____
10. _____

Date: _____

1. _____
2. _____
3. _____
4. _____
5. _____
6. _____
7. _____
8. _____
9. _____
10. _____

Date: _____

1. _____
2. _____
3. _____
4. _____
5. _____
6. _____
7. _____
8. _____
9. _____
10. _____

Date: _____

1. _____
2. _____
3. _____
4. _____
5. _____
6. _____
7. _____
8. _____
9. _____
10. _____

Date: _____

1. _____
2. _____
3. _____
4. _____
5. _____
6. _____
7. _____
8. _____
9. _____
10. _____

Date: _____

1. _____
2. _____
3. _____
4. _____
5. _____
6. _____
7. _____
8. _____
9. _____
10. _____

10 *BEFORE* 10 **GRATITUDE** LIST

Take note of 10 things you're grateful for before 10am

Date: _____

1. _____   6. _____
2. _____   7. _____
3. _____   8. _____
4. _____   9. _____
5. _____   10. _____

Date: _____

1. _____   6. _____
2. _____   7. _____
3. _____   8. _____
4. _____   9. _____
5. _____   10. _____

Date: _____

1. _____   6. _____
2. _____   7. _____
3. _____   8. _____
4. _____   9. _____
5. _____   10. _____

Date: _____

1. _____   6. _____
2. _____   7. _____
3. _____   8. _____
4. _____   9. _____
5. _____   10. _____

Date: _____

1. _____   6. _____
2. _____   7. _____
3. _____   8. _____
4. _____   9. _____
5. _____   10. _____

Date: _____

1. _____   6. _____
2. _____   7. _____
3. _____   8. _____
4. _____   9. _____
5. _____   10. _____

Date: _____

1. _____   6. _____
2. _____   7. _____
3. _____   8. _____
4. _____   9. _____
5. _____   10. _____

Date: _____

1. _____   6. _____
2. _____   7. _____
3. _____   8. _____
4. _____   9. _____
5. _____   10. _____

Date: _____

1. _____   6. _____
2. _____   7. _____
3. _____   8. _____
4. _____   9. _____
5. _____   10. _____

Date: _____

1. _____   6. _____
2. _____   7. _____
3. _____   8. _____
4. _____   9. _____
5. _____   10. _____

Date: _____

1. _____   6. _____
2. _____   7. _____
3. _____   8. _____
4. _____   9. _____
5. _____   10. _____

Date: _____

1. _____   6. _____
2. _____   7. _____
3. _____   8. _____
4. _____   9. _____
5. _____   10. _____

10 BEFORE 10 GRATITUDE LIST

Take note of 10 things you're grateful for before 10am

Date: _____

1. _____   6. _____
2. _____   7. _____
3. _____   8. _____
4. _____   9. _____
5. _____   10. _____

Date: _____

1. _____   6. _____
2. _____   7. _____
3. _____   8. _____
4. _____   9. _____
5. _____   10. _____

Date: _____

1. _____   6. _____
2. _____   7. _____
3. _____   8. _____
4. _____   9. _____
5. _____   10. _____

Date: _____

1. _____   6. _____
2. _____   7. _____
3. _____   8. _____
4. _____   9. _____
5. _____   10. _____

Date: _____

1. _____   6. _____
2. _____   7. _____
3. _____   8. _____
4. _____   9. _____
5. _____   10. _____

Date: _____

1. _____   6. _____
2. _____   7. _____
3. _____   8. _____
4. _____   9. _____
5. _____   10. _____

Date: _____

1. _____   6. _____
2. _____   7. _____
3. _____   8. _____
4. _____   9. _____
5. _____   10. _____

Date: _____

1. _____   6. _____
2. _____   7. _____
3. _____   8. _____
4. _____   9. _____
5. _____   10. _____

Date: _____

1. _____   6. _____
2. _____   7. _____
3. _____   8. _____
4. _____   9. _____
5. _____   10. _____

Date: _____

1. _____   6. _____
2. _____   7. _____
3. _____   8. _____
4. _____   9. _____
5. _____   10. _____

Date: _____

1. _____   6. _____
2. _____   7. _____
3. _____   8. _____
4. _____   9. _____
5. _____   10. _____

Date: _____

1. _____   6. _____
2. _____   7. _____
3. _____   8. _____
4. _____   9. _____
5. _____   10. _____

Date: _____

1. _____   6. _____
2. _____   7. _____
3. _____   8. _____
4. _____   9. _____
5. _____   10. _____

Date: _____

1. _____   6. _____
2. _____   7. _____
3. _____   8. _____
4. _____   9. _____
5. _____   10. _____

10 BEFORE 10 GRATITUDE LIST

Take note of 10 things you're grateful for before 10am

Date: _____

1. _____   6. _____
2. _____   7. _____
3. _____   8. _____
4. _____   9. _____
5. _____   10. _____

Date: _____

1. _____   6. _____
2. _____   7. _____
3. _____   8. _____
4. _____   9. _____
5. _____   10. _____

Date: _____

1. _____   6. _____
2. _____   7. _____
3. _____   8. _____
4. _____   9. _____
5. _____   10. _____

Date: _____

1. _____   6. _____
2. _____   7. _____
3. _____   8. _____
4. _____   9. _____
5. _____   10. _____

Date: _____

1. _____   6. _____
2. _____   7. _____
3. _____   8. _____
4. _____   9. _____
5. _____   10. _____

Date: _____

1. _____   6. _____
2. _____   7. _____
3. _____   8. _____
4. _____   9. _____
5. _____   10. _____

Date: _____

1. _____   6. _____
2. _____   7. _____
3. _____   8. _____
4. _____   9. _____
5. _____   10. _____

Date: _____

1. _____   6. _____
2. _____   7. _____
3. _____   8. _____
4. _____   9. _____
5. _____   10. _____

Date: _____

1. _____   6. _____
2. _____   7. _____
3. _____   8. _____
4. _____   9. _____
5. _____   10. _____

Date: _____

1. _____   6. _____
2. _____   7. _____
3. _____   8. _____
4. _____   9. _____
5. _____   10. _____

Date: _____

1. _____   6. _____
2. _____   7. _____
3. _____   8. _____
4. _____   9. _____
5. _____   10. _____

Date: _____

1. _____   6. _____
2. _____   7. _____
3. _____   8. _____
4. _____   9. _____
5. _____   10. _____

Date: _____

1. _____   6. _____
2. _____   7. _____
3. _____   8. _____
4. _____   9. _____
5. _____   10. _____

Date: _____

1. _____   6. _____
2. _____   7. _____
3. _____   8. _____
4. _____   9. _____
5. _____   10. _____

10 *BEFORE* 10 **GRATITUDE** LIST

Take note of 10 things you're grateful for before 10am

Date: _____

1. _____   6. _____
2. _____   7. _____
3. _____   8. _____
4. _____   9. _____
5. _____   10. _____

Date: _____

1. _____   6. _____
2. _____   7. _____
3. _____   8. _____
4. _____   9. _____
5. _____   10. _____

Date: _____

1. _____   6. _____
2. _____   7. _____
3. _____   8. _____
4. _____   9. _____
5. _____   10. _____

Date: _____

1. _____   6. _____
2. _____   7. _____
3. _____   8. _____
4. _____   9. _____
5. _____   10. _____

Date: _____

1. _____   6. _____
2. _____   7. _____
3. _____   8. _____
4. _____   9. _____
5. _____   10. _____

Date: _____

1. _____   6. _____
2. _____   7. _____
3. _____   8. _____
4. _____   9. _____
5. _____   10. _____

Date: _____

1. _____   6. _____
2. _____   7. _____
3. _____   8. _____
4. _____   9. _____
5. _____   10. _____

Date: _____

1. _____   6. _____
2. _____   7. _____
3. _____   8. _____
4. _____   9. _____
5. _____   10. _____

Date: _____

1. _____   6. _____
2. _____   7. _____
3. _____   8. _____
4. _____   9. _____
5. _____   10. _____

Date: _____

1. _____   6. _____
2. _____   7. _____
3. _____   8. _____
4. _____   9. _____
5. _____   10. _____

Date: _____

1. _____   6. _____
2. _____   7. _____
3. _____   8. _____
4. _____   9. _____
5. _____   10. _____

Date: _____

1. _____   6. _____
2. _____   7. _____
3. _____   8. _____
4. _____   9. _____
5. _____   10. _____

10 *BEFORE* 10 **GRATITUDE** LIST

Take note of 10 things you're grateful for before 10am

Date: _____

1. _____	6. _____
2. _____	7. _____
3. _____	8. _____
4. _____	9. _____
5. _____	10. _____

Date: _____

1. _____	6. _____
2. _____	7. _____
3. _____	8. _____
4. _____	9. _____
5. _____	10. _____

Date: _____

1. _____	6. _____
2. _____	7. _____
3. _____	8. _____
4. _____	9. _____
5. _____	10. _____

Date: _____

1. _____	6. _____
2. _____	7. _____
3. _____	8. _____
4. _____	9. _____
5. _____	10. _____

Date: _____

1. _____	6. _____
2. _____	7. _____
3. _____	8. _____
4. _____	9. _____
5. _____	10. _____

Date: _____

1. _____	6. _____
2. _____	7. _____
3. _____	8. _____
4. _____	9. _____
5. _____	10. _____

Date: _____

1. _____	6. _____
2. _____	7. _____
3. _____	8. _____
4. _____	9. _____
5. _____	10. _____

Date: _____

1. _____	6. _____
2. _____	7. _____
3. _____	8. _____
4. _____	9. _____
5. _____	10. _____

Date: _____

1. _____	6. _____
2. _____	7. _____
3. _____	8. _____
4. _____	9. _____
5. _____	10. _____

Date: _____

1. _____	6. _____
2. _____	7. _____
3. _____	8. _____
4. _____	9. _____
5. _____	10. _____

Date: _____

1. _____	6. _____
2. _____	7. _____
3. _____	8. _____
4. _____	9. _____
5. _____	10. _____

Date: _____

1. _____	6. _____
2. _____	7. _____
3. _____	8. _____
4. _____	9. _____
5. _____	10. _____

Date: _____

1. _____	6. _____
2. _____	7. _____
3. _____	8. _____
4. _____	9. _____
5. _____	10. _____

Date: _____

1. _____	6. _____
2. _____	7. _____
3. _____	8. _____
4. _____	9. _____
5. _____	10. _____

10 *BEFORE* 10 **GRATITUDE** LIST

Date: _____

1. _____   6. _____
2. _____   7. _____
3. _____   8. _____
4. _____   9. _____
5. _____   10. _____

Date: _____

1. _____   6. _____
2. _____   7. _____
3. _____   8. _____
4. _____   9. _____
5. _____   10. _____

Date: _____

1. _____   6. _____
2. _____   7. _____
3. _____   8. _____
4. _____   9. _____
5. _____   10. _____

Date: _____

1. _____   6. _____
2. _____   7. _____
3. _____   8. _____
4. _____   9. _____
5. _____   10. _____

Date: _____

1. _____   6. _____
2. _____   7. _____
3. _____   8. _____
4. _____   9. _____
5. _____   10. _____

Date: _____

1. _____   6. _____
2. _____   7. _____
3. _____   8. _____
4. _____   9. _____
5. _____   10. _____

Date: _____

1. _____   6. _____
2. _____   7. _____
3. _____   8. _____
4. _____   9. _____
5. _____   10. _____

Date: _____

1. _____   6. _____
2. _____   7. _____
3. _____   8. _____
4. _____   9. _____
5. _____   10. _____

Date: _____

1. _____   6. _____
2. _____   7. _____
3. _____   8. _____
4. _____   9. _____
5. _____   10. _____

Date: _____

1. _____   6. _____
2. _____   7. _____
3. _____   8. _____
4. _____   9. _____
5. _____   10. _____

Date: _____

1. _____   6. _____
2. _____   7. _____
3. _____   8. _____
4. _____   9. _____
5. _____   10. _____

Date: _____

1. _____   6. _____
2. _____   7. _____
3. _____   8. _____
4. _____   9. _____
5. _____   10. _____

Date: _____

1. _____   6. _____
2. _____   7. _____
3. _____   8. _____
4. _____   9. _____
5. _____   10. _____

Date: _____

1. _____   6. _____
2. _____   7. _____
3. _____   8. _____
4. _____   9. _____
5. _____   10. _____

10 *BEFORE* 10 **GRATITUDE** LIST

Date: _____

1. _____   6. _____
2. _____   7. _____
3. _____   8. _____
4. _____   9. _____
5. _____   10. _____

Date: _____

1. _____   6. _____
2. _____   7. _____
3. _____   8. _____
4. _____   9. _____
5. _____   10. _____

Date: _____

1. _____   6. _____
2. _____   7. _____
3. _____   8. _____
4. _____   9. _____
5. _____   10. _____

Date: _____

1. _____   6. _____
2. _____   7. _____
3. _____   8. _____
4. _____   9. _____
5. _____   10. _____

Date: _____

1. _____   6. _____
2. _____   7. _____
3. _____   8. _____
4. _____   9. _____
5. _____   10. _____

Date: _____

1. _____   6. _____
2. _____   7. _____
3. _____   8. _____
4. _____   9. _____
5. _____   10. _____

Date: _____

1. _____   6. _____
2. _____   7. _____
3. _____   8. _____
4. _____   9. _____
5. _____   10. _____

Date: _____

1. _____   6. _____
2. _____   7. _____
3. _____   8. _____
4. _____   9. _____
5. _____   10. _____

Date: _____

1. _____   6. _____
2. _____   7. _____
3. _____   8. _____
4. _____   9. _____
5. _____   10. _____

Date: _____

1. _____   6. _____
2. _____   7. _____
3. _____   8. _____
4. _____   9. _____
5. _____   10. _____

Date: _____

1. _____   6. _____
2. _____   7. _____
3. _____   8. _____
4. _____   9. _____
5. _____   10. _____

Date: _____

1. _____   6. _____
2. _____   7. _____
3. _____   8. _____
4. _____   9. _____
5. _____   10. _____

10 BEFORE 10 GRATITUDE LIST

Take note of 10 things you're grateful for before 10am

Date: _____

1. _____
2. _____
3. _____
4. _____
5. _____

6. _____
7. _____
8. _____
9. _____
10. _____

Date: _____

1. _____
2. _____
3. _____
4. _____
5. _____

6. _____
7. _____
8. _____
9. _____
10. _____

Date: _____

1. _____
2. _____
3. _____
4. _____
5. _____

6. _____
7. _____
8. _____
9. _____
10. _____

Date: _____

1. _____
2. _____
3. _____
4. _____
5. _____

6. _____
7. _____
8. _____
9. _____
10. _____

Date: _____

1. _____
2. _____
3. _____
4. _____
5. _____

6. _____
7. _____
8. _____
9. _____
10. _____

Date: _____

1. _____
2. _____
3. _____
4. _____
5. _____

6. _____
7. _____
8. _____
9. _____
10. _____

Date: _____

1. _____
2. _____
3. _____
4. _____
5. _____

6. _____
7. _____
8. _____
9. _____
10. _____

Date: _____

1. _____
2. _____
3. _____
4. _____
5. _____

6. _____
7. _____
8. _____
9. _____
10. _____

Date: _____

1. _____
2. _____
3. _____
4. _____
5. _____

6. _____
7. _____
8. _____
9. _____
10. _____

Date: _____

1. _____
2. _____
3. _____
4. _____
5. _____

6. _____
7. _____
8. _____
9. _____
10. _____

Date: _____

1. _____
2. _____
3. _____
4. _____
5. _____

6. _____
7. _____
8. _____
9. _____
10. _____

Date: _____

1. _____
2. _____
3. _____
4. _____
5. _____

6. _____
7. _____
8. _____
9. _____
10. _____

Date: _____

1. _____
2. _____
3. _____
4. _____
5. _____

6. _____
7. _____
8. _____
9. _____
10. _____

Date: _____

1. _____
2. _____
3. _____
4. _____
5. _____

6. _____
7. _____
8. _____
9. _____
10. _____

WEEK OF
/ / - / /

THIS WEEK'S GOAL / FOCUS

WHAT DO I NEED TO...

STOP _____
_____

START _____
_____

CONTINUE _____
_____

QUOTE OF THE WEEK
"You can get everything in life you want if you will just help enough other people get what they want."
ZIG ZIGLAR

DECLARATION OF THE WEEK
Every day in every way I am getting better and better.

WRITE YOUR OWN DECLARATIONS FOR THIS WEEK BELOW:
_____
_____
_____
_____
_____
_____
_____
_____
_____
_____
_____
_____
_____
_____
_____
_____
_____
_____
_____
_____
_____

MAXIMIZE YOUR LIFE PLANNER

MAKE IT HAPPEN **MONDAY** ☐	*TAKE ACTION* **TUESDAY** ☐	*WHATEVER IT TAKES* **WEDNESDAY** ☐
TODAY'S GOAL	TODAY'S GOAL	TODAY'S GOAL
5:00	5:00	5:00
5:30	5:30	5:30
6:00	6:00	6:00
6:30	6:30	6:30
7:00	7:00	7:00
7:30	7:30	7:30
8:00	8:00	8:00
8:30	8:30	8:30
9:00	9:00	9:00
9:30	9:30	9:30
10:00	10:00	10:00
10:30	10:30	10:30
11:00	11:00	11:00
11:30	11:30	11:30
12:00	12:00	12:00
12:30	12:30	12:30
1:00	1:00	1:00
1:30	1:30	1:30
2:00	2:00	2:00
2:30	2:30	2:30
3:00	3:00	3:00
3:30	3:30	3:30
4:00	4:00	4:00
4:30	4:30	4:30
5:00	5:00	5:00
5:30	5:30	5:30
6:00	6:00	6:00
6:30	6:30	6:30
7:00	7:00	7:00
7:30	7:30	7:30
8:00	8:00	8:00
8:30	8:30	8:30
9:00	9:00	9:00
9:30	9:30	9:30
10:00	10:00	10:00
10:30	10:30	10:30
11:00	11:00	11:00
11:30	11:30	11:30
12:00	12:00	12:00
12:30	12:30	12:30

PERSONAL TO-DO LIST	**WORK** TO-DO LIST	**FOLLOW UP** LIST
☐	☐	/
☐	☐	/
☐	☐	/
☐	☐	/
☐	☐	/
☐	☐	/
☐	☐	/
☐	☐	/
☐	☐	/

THURSDAY	FRIDAY	SATURDAY	SUNDAY
TODAY'S GOAL	TODAY'S GOAL	TODAY'S GOAL	TODAY'S GOAL

	THURSDAY		FRIDAY		SATURDAY		SUNDAY
5:00		5:00		5:00		5:00	
5:30		5:30		5:30		5:30	
6:00		6:00		6:00		6:00	
6:30		6:30		6:30		6:30	
7:00		7:00		7:00		7:00	
7:30		7:30		7:30		7:30	
8:00		8:00		8:00		8:00	
8:30		8:30		8:30		8:30	
9:00		9:00		9:00		9:00	
9:30		9:30		9:30		9:30	
10:00		10:00		10:00		10:00	
10:30		10:30		10:30		10:30	
11:00		11:00		11:00		11:00	
11:30		11:30		11:30		11:30	
12:00		12:00		12:00		12:00	
12:30		12:30		12:30		12:30	
1:00		1:00		1:00		1:00	
1:30		1:30		1:30		1:30	
2:00		2:00		2:00		2:00	
2:30		2:30		2:30		2:30	
3:00		3:00		3:00		3:00	
3:30		3:30		3:30		3:30	
4:00		4:00		4:00		4:00	
4:30		4:30		4:30		4:30	
5:00		5:00		5:00		5:00	
5:30		5:30		5:30		5:30	
6:00		6:00		6:00		6:00	
6:30		6:30		6:30		6:30	
7:00		7:00		7:00		7:00	
7:30		7:30		7:30		7:30	
8:00		8:00		8:00		8:00	
8:30		8:30		8:30		8:30	
9:00		9:00		9:00		9:00	
9:30		9:30		9:30		9:30	
10:00		10:00		10:00		10:00	
10:30		10:30		10:30		10:30	
11:00		11:00		11:00		11:00	
11:30		11:30		11:30		11:30	
12:00		12:00		12:00		12:00	
12:30		12:30		12:30		12:30	

We are what we repeatedly do... *Excellence, then is* *NOT an act, but a HABIT!*	MON	TUES	WED	THURS	FRI	SAT	SUN
10 *BEFORE* **10 GRATITUDE**							
DECLARATIONS							
AUDIO							
READ							
FITNESS							
CONTACT 5 *BY* **5**							

THOUGHTS / IDEAS / VISIONS / DREAMS

WEEK OF

_____ / _____ - _____ / _____

WHAT DO I NEED TO...

STOP _____

_____

START _____

_____

CONTINUE _____

_____

QUOTE OF THE WEEK

"Someone's sitting in the shade today because someone planted a tree a long time ago."
WARREN BUFFET

DECLARATION OF THE WEEK

I am a success magnet, and attract success in everything I do.

WRITE YOUR OWN DECLARATIONS FOR THIS WEEK BELOW:

_____
_____
_____
_____
_____
_____
_____
_____
_____
_____
_____
_____
_____
_____
_____
_____
_____
_____

MAXIMIZE YOUR LIFE
P L A N N E R

MAKE IT HAPPEN **MONDAY** ☐	TAKE ACTION **TUESDAY** ☐	WHATEVER IT TAKES **WEDNESDAY** ☐
TODAY'S GOAL	TODAY'S GOAL	TODAY'S GOAL
5:00	5:00	5:00
5:30	5:30	5:30
6:00	6:00	6:00
6:30	6:30	6:30
7:00	7:00	7:00
7:30	7:30	7:30
8:00	8:00	8:00
8:30	8:30	8:30
9:00	9:00	9:00
9:30	9:30	9:30
10:00	10:00	10:00
10:30	10:30	10:30
11:00	11:00	11:00
11:30	11:30	11:30
12:00	12:00	12:00
12:30	12:30	12:30
1:00	1:00	1:00
1:30	1:30	1:30
2:00	2:00	2:00
2:30	2:30	2:30
3:00	3:00	3:00
3:30	3:30	3:30
4:00	4:00	4:00
4:30	4:30	4:30
5:00	5:00	5:00
5:30	5:30	5:30
6:00	6:00	6:00
6:30	6:30	6:30
7:00	7:00	7:00
7:30	7:30	7:30
8:00	8:00	8:00
8:30	8:30	8:30
9:00	9:00	9:00
9:30	9:30	9:30
10:00	10:00	10:00
10:30	10:30	10:30
11:00	11:00	11:00
11:30	11:30	11:30
12:00	12:00	12:00
12:30	12:30	12:30

PERSONAL TO-DO LIST	**WORK** TO-DO LIST	**FOLLOW UP** LIST
☐	☐	/
☐	☐	/
☐	☐	/
☐	☐	/
☐	☐	/
☐	☐	/
☐	☐	/
☐	☐	/
☐	☐	/

THURSDAY	FRIDAY	SATURDAY	SUNDAY
TODAY'S GOAL	TODAY'S GOAL	TODAY'S GOAL	TODAY'S GOAL
5:00	5:00	5:00	5:00
5:30	5:30	5:30	5:30
6:00	6:00	6:00	6:00
6:30	6:30	6:30	6:30
7:00	7:00	7:00	7:00
7:30	7:30	7:30	7:30
8:00	8:00	8:00	8:00
8:30	8:30	8:30	8:30
9:00	9:00	9:00	9:00
9:30	9:30	9:30	9:30
10:00	10:00	10:00	10:00
10:30	10:30	10:30	10:30
11:00	11:00	11:00	11:00
11:30	11:30	11:30	11:30
12:00	12:00	12:00	12:00
12:30	12:30	12:30	12:30
1:00	1:00	1:00	1:00
1:30	1:30	1:30	1:30
2:00	2:00	2:00	2:00
2:30	2:30	2:30	2:30
3:00	3:00	3:00	3:00
3:30	3:30	3:30	3:30
4:00	4:00	4:00	4:00
4:30	4:30	4:30	4:30
5:00	5:00	5:00	5:00
5:30	5:30	5:30	5:30
6:00	6:00	6:00	6:00
6:30	6:30	6:30	6:30
7:00	7:00	7:00	7:00
7:30	7:30	7:30	7:30
8:00	8:00	8:00	8:00
8:30	8:30	8:30	8:30
9:00	9:00	9:00	9:00
9:30	9:30	9:30	9:30
10:00	10:00	10:00	10:00
10:30	10:30	10:30	10:30
11:00	11:00	11:00	11:00
11:30	11:30	11:30	11:30
12:00	12:00	12:00	12:00
12:30	12:30	12:30	12:30

We are what we repeatedly do... Excellence, then is NOT an act, but a HABIT!

	MON	TUES	WED	THURS	FRI	SAT	SUN
10 *BEFORE* 10 GRATITUDE							
DECLARATIONS							
AUDIO							
READ							
FITNESS							
CONTACT 5 *BY* 5							

THOUGHTS / IDEAS / VISIONS / DREAMS

WEEK OF
/ / - / /

THIS WEEK'S GOAL / FOCUS

WHAT DO I NEED TO...

STOP _____
_____

START _____
_____

CONTINUE _____
_____

QUOTE OF THE WEEK

"Life can be much broader once you discover one simple fact: Everything around you that you call life was made up by people that were no smarter than you. And you can change it, you can influence it… Once you learn that, you'll never be the same again."
STEVE JOBS

DECLARATION OF THE WEEK

My ability to conquer my challenges is limitless, and my potential to succeed is infinite.

WRITE YOUR OWN DECLARATIONS FOR THIS WEEK BELOW:

_____
_____
_____
_____
_____
_____
_____
_____
_____
_____
_____
_____
_____
_____

MAXIMIZE YOUR LIFE PLANNER

MAKE IT HAPPEN MONDAY ☐	TAKE ACTION TUESDAY ☐	WHATEVER IT TAKES WEDNESDAY ☐
TODAY'S GOAL	TODAY'S GOAL	TODAY'S GOAL
5:00	5:00	5:00
5:30	5:30	5:30
6:00	6:00	6:00
6:30	6:30	6:30
7:00	7:00	7:00
7:30	7:30	7:30
8:00	8:00	8:00
8:30	8:30	8:30
9:00	9:00	9:00
9:30	9:30	9:30
10:00	10:00	10:00
10:30	10:30	10:30
11:00	11:00	11:00
11:30	11:30	11:30
12:00	12:00	12:00
12:30	12:30	12:30
1:00	1:00	1:00
1:30	1:30	1:30
2:00	2:00	2:00
2:30	2:30	2:30
3:00	3:00	3:00
3:30	3:30	3:30
4:00	4:00	4:00
4:30	4:30	4:30
5:00	5:00	5:00
5:30	5:30	5:30
6:00	6:00	6:00
6:30	6:30	6:30
7:00	7:00	7:00
7:30	7:30	7:30
8:00	8:00	8:00
8:30	8:30	8:30
9:00	9:00	9:00
9:30	9:30	9:30
10:00	10:00	10:00
10:30	10:30	10:30
11:00	11:00	11:00
11:30	11:30	11:30
12:00	12:00	12:00
12:30	12:30	12:30
PERSONAL TO-DO LIST	**WORK** TO-DO LIST	**FOLLOW UP** LIST
☐	☐	/
☐	☐	/
☐	☐	/
☐	☐	/
☐	☐	/
☐	☐	/
☐	☐	/
☐	☐	/
☐	☐	/

TODAY'S GOAL | **TODAY'S GOAL** | **TODAY'S GOAL** | **TODAY'S GOAL**

THURSDAY	FRIDAY	SATURDAY	SUNDAY
5:00	5:00	5:00	5:00
5:30	5:30	5:30	5:30
6:00	6:00	6:00	6:00
6:30	6:30	6:30	6:30
7:00	7:00	7:00	7:00
7:30	7:30	7:30	7:30
8:00	8:00	8:00	8:00
8:30	8:30	8:30	8:30
9:00	9:00	9:00	9:00
9:30	9:30	9:30	9:30
10:00	10:00	10:00	10:00
10:30	10:30	10:30	10:30
11:00	11:00	11:00	11:00
11:30	11:30	11:30	11:30
12:00	12:00	12:00	12:00
12:30	12:30	12:30	12:30
1:00	1:00	1:00	1:00
1:30	1:30	1:30	1:30
2:00	2:00	2:00	2:00
2:30	2:30	2:30	2:30
3:00	3:00	3:00	3:00
3:30	3:30	3:30	3:30
4:00	4:00	4:00	4:00
4:30	4:30	4:30	4:30
5:00	5:00	5:00	5:00
5:30	5:30	5:30	5:30
6:00	6:00	6:00	6:00
6:30	6:30	6:30	6:30
7:00	7:00	7:00	7:00
7:30	7:30	7:30	7:30
8:00	8:00	8:00	8:00
8:30	8:30	8:30	8:30
9:00	9:00	9:00	9:00
9:30	9:30	9:30	9:30
10:00	10:00	10:00	10:00
10:30	10:30	10:30	10:30
11:00	11:00	11:00	11:00
11:30	11:30	11:30	11:30
12:00	12:00	12:00	12:00
12:30	12:30	12:30	12:30

We are what we repeatedly do... Excellence, then is NOT an act, but a HABIT!	MON	TUES	WED	THURS	FRI	SAT	SUN
10 *BEFORE* 10 GRATITUDE							
DECLARATIONS							
AUDIO							
READ							
FITNESS							
CONTACT 5 *BY* 5							

THOUGHTS / IDEAS / VISIONS / DREAMS

WEEK OF
/ / - / /

THIS WEEK'S GOAL / FOCUS

WHAT DO I NEED TO...

STOP _____

_____

START _____

_____

CONTINUE _____

_____

QUOTE OF THE WEEK

"Life is like riding a bicycle. To keep your balance you must keep moving."
ALBERT EINSTEIN

DECLARATION OF THE WEEK

I am so happy and grateful now that I am living an abundant lifestyle, and enjoying every moment of it.

WRITE YOUR OWN DECLARATIONS FOR THIS WEEK BELOW:

_____
_____
_____
_____
_____
_____
_____
_____
_____
_____
_____
_____
_____
_____
_____
_____
_____
_____

MAXIMIZE YOUR LIFE PLANNER

MAKE IT HAPPEN **MONDAY** ☐	TAKE ACTION **TUESDAY** ☐	WHATEVER IT TAKES **WEDNESDAY** ☐
TODAY'S GOAL	TODAY'S GOAL	TODAY'S GOAL
5:00	5:00	5:00
5:30	5:30	5:30
6:00	6:00	6:00
6:30	6:30	6:30
7:00	7:00	7:00
7:30	7:30	7:30
8:00	8:00	8:00
8:30	8:30	8:30
9:00	9:00	9:00
9:30	9:30	9:30
10:00	10:00	10:00
10:30	10:30	10:30
11:00	11:00	11:00
11:30	11:30	11:30
12:00	12:00	12:00
12:30	12:30	12:30
1:00	1:00	1:00
1:30	1:30	1:30
2:00	2:00	2:00
2:30	2:30	2:30
3:00	3:00	3:00
3:30	3:30	3:30
4:00	4:00	4:00
4:30	4:30	4:30
5:00	5:00	5:00
5:30	5:30	5:30
6:00	6:00	6:00
6:30	6:30	6:30
7:00	7:00	7:00
7:30	7:30	7:30
8:00	8:00	8:00
8:30	8:30	8:30
9:00	9:00	9:00
9:30	9:30	9:30
10:00	10:00	10:00
10:30	10:30	10:30
11:00	11:00	11:00
11:30	11:30	11:30
12:00	12:00	12:00
12:30	12:30	12:30
PERSONAL TO-DO LIST	**WORK** TO-DO LIST	**FOLLOW UP** LIST
☐	☐	/
☐	☐	/
☐	☐	/
☐	☐	/
☐	☐	/
☐	☐	/
☐	☐	/
☐	☐	/
☐	☐	/

TODAY'S GOAL	TODAY'S GOAL	TODAY'S GOAL	TODAY'S GOAL
5:00	5:00	5:00	5:00
5:30	5:30	5:30	5:30
6:00	6:00	6:00	6:00
6:30	6:30	6:30	6:30
7:00	7:00	7:00	7:00
7:30	7:30	7:30	7:30
8:00	8:00	8:00	8:00
8:30	8:30	8:30	8:30
9:00	9:00	9:00	9:00
9:30	9:30	9:30	9:30
10:00	10:00	10:00	10:00
10:30	10:30	10:30	10:30
11:00	11:00	11:00	11:00
11:30	11:30	11:30	11:30
12:00	12:00	12:00	12:00
12:30	12:30	12:30	12:30
1:00	1:00	1:00	1:00
1:30	1:30	1:30	1:30
2:00	2:00	2:00	2:00
2:30	2:30	2:30	2:30
3:00	3:00	3:00	3:00
3:30	3:30	3:30	3:30
4:00	4:00	4:00	4:00
4:30	4:30	4:30	4:30
5:00	5:00	5:00	5:00
5:30	5:30	5:30	5:30
6:00	6:00	6:00	6:00
6:30	6:30	6:30	6:30
7:00	7:00	7:00	7:00
7:30	7:30	7:30	7:30
8:00	8:00	8:00	8:00
8:30	8:30	8:30	8:30
9:00	9:00	9:00	9:00
9:30	9:30	9:30	9:30
10:00	10:00	10:00	10:00
10:30	10:30	10:30	10:30
11:00	11:00	11:00	11:00
11:30	11:30	11:30	11:30
12:00	12:00	12:00	12:00
12:30	12:30	12:30	12:30

We are what we repeatedly do... Excellence, then is NOT an act, but a HABIT!

	MON	TUES	WED	THURS	FRI	SAT	SUN
10 *BEFORE* 10 GRATITUDE							
DECLARATIONS							
AUDIO							
READ							
FITNESS							
CONTACT 5 *BY* 5							

THOUGHTS / IDEAS / VISIONS / DREAMS

WEEK OF

/ / - / /

THIS WEEK'S GOAL / FOCUS

WHAT DO I NEED TO...

STOP _____

_____

START _____

_____

CONTINUE _____

_____

QUOTE OF THE WEEK

"Live as if you were to die tomorrow. Learn as if you were to live forever."
MAHATMA GANDHI

DECLARATION OF THE WEEK

I am at peace with myself and the world, and everything is going smoothly in my life.

WRITE YOUR OWN DECLARATIONS FOR THIS WEEK BELOW:

_____
_____
_____
_____
_____
_____
_____
_____
_____
_____
_____
_____
_____
_____
_____
_____
_____

MAXIMIZE
YOUR LIFE
P L A N N E R

MAKE IT HAPPEN **MONDAY** ☐	*TAKE ACTION* **TUESDAY** ☐	*WHATEVER IT TAKES* **WEDNESDAY** ☐
TODAY'S GOAL	TODAY'S GOAL	TODAY'S GOAL
5:00	5:00	5:00
5:30	5:30	5:30
6:00	6:00	6:00
6:30	6:30	6:30
7:00	7:00	7:00
7:30	7:30	7:30
8:00	8:00	8:00
8:30	8:30	8:30
9:00	9:00	9:00
9:30	9:30	9:30
10:00	10:00	10:00
10:30	10:30	10:30
11:00	11:00	11:00
11:30	11:30	11:30
12:00	12:00	12:00
12:30	12:30	12:30
1:00	1:00	1:00
1:30	1:30	1:30
2:00	2:00	2:00
2:30	2:30	2:30
3:00	3:00	3:00
3:30	3:30	3:30
4:00	4:00	4:00
4:30	4:30	4:30
5:00	5:00	5:00
5:30	5:30	5:30
6:00	6:00	6:00
6:30	6:30	6:30
7:00	7:00	7:00
7:30	7:30	7:30
8:00	8:00	8:00
8:30	8:30	8:30
9:00	9:00	9:00
9:30	9:30	9:30
10:00	10:00	10:00
10:30	10:30	10:30
11:00	11:00	11:00
11:30	11:30	11:30
12:00	12:00	12:00
12:30	12:30	12:30
PERSONAL TO-DO LIST	**WORK** TO-DO LIST	**FOLLOW UP** LIST
☐	☐	/
☐	☐	/
☐	☐	/
☐	☐	/
☐	☐	/
☐	☐	/
☐	☐	/
☐	☐	/
☐	☐	/

TURN IT UP
THURSDAY ☐

FINISH STRONG
FRIDAY ☐

STEP IT UP
SATURDAY ☐

SOULFUL
SUNDAY ☐

TODAY'S GOAL	TODAY'S GOAL	TODAY'S GOAL	TODAY'S GOAL

THURSDAY	FRIDAY	SATURDAY	SUNDAY
5:00	5:00	5:00	5:00
5:30	5:30	5:30	5:30
6:00	6:00	6:00	6:00
6:30	6:30	6:30	6:30
7:00	7:00	7:00	7:00
7:30	7:30	7:30	7:30
8:00	8:00	8:00	8:00
8:30	8:30	8:30	8:30
9:00	9:00	9:00	9:00
9:30	9:30	9:30	9:30
10:00	10:00	10:00	10:00
10:30	10:30	10:30	10:30
11:00	11:00	11:00	11:00
11:30	11:30	11:30	11:30
12:00	12:00	12:00	12:00
12:30	12:30	12:30	12:30
1:00	1:00	1:00	1:00
1:30	1:30	1:30	1:30
2:00	2:00	2:00	2:00
2:30	2:30	2:30	2:30
3:00	3:00	3:00	3:00
3:30	3:30	3:30	3:30
4:00	4:00	4:00	4:00
4:30	4:30	4:30	4:30
5:00	5:00	5:00	5:00
5:30	5:30	5:30	5:30
6:00	6:00	6:00	6:00
6:30	6:30	6:30	6:30
7:00	7:00	7:00	7:00
7:30	7:30	7:30	7:30
8:00	8:00	8:00	8:00
8:30	8:30	8:30	8:30
9:00	9:00	9:00	9:00
9:30	9:30	9:30	9:30
10:00	10:00	10:00	10:00
10:30	10:30	10:30	10:30
11:00	11:00	11:00	11:00
11:30	11:30	11:30	11:30
12:00	12:00	12:00	12:00
12:30	12:30	12:30	12:30

We are what we repeatedly do... Excellence, then is NOT an act, but a HABIT!	MON	TUES	WED	THURS	FRI	SAT	SUN
10 *BEFORE* 10 GRATITUDE							
DECLARATIONS							
AUDIO							
READ							
FITNESS							
CONTACT 5 *BY* 5							

THOUGHTS / IDEAS / VISIONS / DREAMS

WEEK OF

/ / - / /

THIS WEEK'S GOAL / FOCUS

WHAT DO I NEED TO...

STOP _____

_____

START _____

_____

CONTINUE _____

_____

QUOTE OF THE WEEK

"The future belongs to those who believe in the beauty of their dreams."
ELEANOR ROOSEVELT

DECLARATION OF THE WEEK

I am wealthy and it feels amazing to contribute to those in need.

WRITE YOUR OWN DECLARATIONS FOR THIS WEEK BELOW:

_____
_____
_____
_____
_____
_____
_____
_____
_____
_____
_____
_____
_____
_____
_____
_____
_____
_____

MAXIMIZE YOUR LIFE PLANNER

MAKE IT HAPPEN MONDAY ☐	TAKE ACTION TUESDAY ☐	WHATEVER IT TAKES WEDNESDAY ☐
TODAY'S GOAL	TODAY'S GOAL	TODAY'S GOAL
5:00	5:00	5:00
5:30	5:30	5:30
6:00	6:00	6:00
6:30	6:30	6:30
7:00	7:00	7:00
7:30	7:30	7:30
8:00	8:00	8:00
8:30	8:30	8:30
9:00	9:00	9:00
9:30	9:30	9:30
10:00	10:00	10:00
10:30	10:30	10:30
11:00	11:00	11:00
11:30	11:30	11:30
12:00	12:00	12:00
12:30	12:30	12:30
1:00	1:00	1:00
1:30	1:30	1:30
2:00	2:00	2:00
2:30	2:30	2:30
3:00	3:00	3:00
3:30	3:30	3:30
4:00	4:00	4:00
4:30	4:30	4:30
5:00	5:00	5:00
5:30	5:30	5:30
6:00	6:00	6:00
6:30	6:30	6:30
7:00	7:00	7:00
7:30	7:30	7:30
8:00	8:00	8:00
8:30	8:30	8:30
9:00	9:00	9:00
9:30	9:30	9:30
10:00	10:00	10:00
10:30	10:30	10:30
11:00	11:00	11:00
11:30	11:30	11:30
12:00	12:00	12:00
12:30	12:30	12:30

PERSONAL TO-DO LIST	WORK TO-DO LIST	FOLLOW UP LIST
☐	☐	/
☐	☐	/
☐	☐	/
☐	☐	/
☐	☐	/
☐	☐	/
☐	☐	/
☐	☐	/
☐	☐	/

TODAY'S GOAL	TODAY'S GOAL	TODAY'S GOAL	TODAY'S GOAL
5:00	5:00	5:00	5:00
5:30	5:30	5:30	5:30
6:00	6:00	6:00	6:00
6:30	6:30	6:30	6:30
7:00	7:00	7:00	7:00
7:30	7:30	7:30	7:30
8:00	8:00	8:00	8:00
8:30	8:30	8:30	8:30
9:00	9:00	9:00	9:00
9:30	9:30	9:30	9:30
10:00	10:00	10:00	10:00
10:30	10:30	10:30	10:30
11:00	11:00	11:00	11:00
11:30	11:30	11:30	11:30
12:00	12:00	12:00	12:00
12:30	12:30	12:30	12:30
1:00	1:00	1:00	1:00
1:30	1:30	1:30	1:30
2:00	2:00	2:00	2:00
2:30	2:30	2:30	2:30
3:00	3:00	3:00	3:00
3:30	3:30	3:30	3:30
4:00	4:00	4:00	4:00
4:30	4:30	4:30	4:30
5:00	5:00	5:00	5:00
5:30	5:30	5:30	5:30
6:00	6:00	6:00	6:00
6:30	6:30	6:30	6:30
7:00	7:00	7:00	7:00
7:30	7:30	7:30	7:30
8:00	8:00	8:00	8:00
8:30	8:30	8:30	8:30
9:00	9:00	9:00	9:00
9:30	9:30	9:30	9:30
10:00	10:00	10:00	10:00
10:30	10:30	10:30	10:30
11:00	11:00	11:00	11:00
11:30	11:30	11:30	11:30
12:00	12:00	12:00	12:00
12:30	12:30	12:30	12:30

We are what we repeatedly do... Excellence, then is NOT an act, but a HABIT!

	MON	TUES	WED	THURS	FRI	SAT	SUN
10 *BEFORE* 10 GRATITUDE							
DECLARATIONS							
AUDIO							
READ							
FITNESS							
CONTACT 5 *BY* 5							

THOUGHTS / IDEAS / VISIONS / DREAMS

WEEK OF

/ / - / /

THIS WEEK'S GOAL / FOCUS

WHAT DO I NEED TO...

STOP _____

_____

START _____

_____

CONTINUE _____

_____

_____

QUOTE OF THE WEEK

"It is our decisions, not our conditions that determine our quality of life."
JOHN C. MAXWELL

DECLARATION OF THE WEEK

I engage in activities that impact this world in a positive way.

WRITE YOUR OWN DECLARATIONS FOR THIS WEEK BELOW:

MAKE IT HAPPEN **MONDAY** ☐	TAKE ACTION **TUESDAY** ☐	WHATEVER IT TAKES **WEDNESDAY** ☐
TODAY'S GOAL	TODAY'S GOAL	TODAY'S GOAL
5:00	5:00	5:00
5:30	5:30	5:30
6:00	6:00	6:00
6:30	6:30	6:30
7:00	7:00	7:00
7:30	7:30	7:30
8:00	8:00	8:00
8:30	8:30	8:30
9:00	9:00	9:00
9:30	9:30	9:30
10:00	10:00	10:00
10:30	10:30	10:30
11:00	11:00	11:00
11:30	11:30	11:30
12:00	12:00	12:00
12:30	12:30	12:30
1:00	1:00	1:00
1:30	1:30	1:30
2:00	2:00	2:00
2:30	2:30	2:30
3:00	3:00	3:00
3:30	3:30	3:30
4:00	4:00	4:00
4:30	4:30	4:30
5:00	5:00	5:00
5:30	5:30	5:30
6:00	6:00	6:00
6:30	6:30	6:30
7:00	7:00	7:00
7:30	7:30	7:30
8:00	8:00	8:00
8:30	8:30	8:30
9:00	9:00	9:00
9:30	9:30	9:30
10:00	10:00	10:00
10:30	10:30	10:30
11:00	11:00	11:00
11:30	11:30	11:30
12:00	12:00	12:00
12:30	12:30	12:30
PERSONAL TO-DO LIST	**WORK** TO-DO LIST	**FOLLOW UP** LIST
☐	☐	/
☐	☐	/
☐	☐	/
☐	☐	/
☐	☐	/
☐	☐	/
☐	☐	/
☐	☐	/
☐	☐	/

MAXIMIZE YOUR LIFE
P L A N N E R

TURN IT UP
THURSDAY ☐
TODAY'S GOAL

Time	
5:00	
5:30	
6:00	
6:30	
7:00	
7:30	
8:00	
8:30	
9:00	
9:30	
10:00	
10:30	
11:00	
11:30	
12:00	
12:30	
1:00	
1:30	
2:00	
2:30	
3:00	
3:30	
4:00	
4:30	
5:00	
5:30	
6:00	
6:30	
7:00	
7:30	
8:00	
8:30	
9:00	
9:30	
10:00	
10:30	
11:00	
11:30	
12:00	
12:30	

FINISH STRONG
FRIDAY ☐
TODAY'S GOAL

Time	
5:00	
5:30	
6:00	
6:30	
7:00	
7:30	
8:00	
8:30	
9:00	
9:30	
10:00	
10:30	
11:00	
11:30	
12:00	
12:30	
1:00	
1:30	
2:00	
2:30	
3:00	
3:30	
4:00	
4:30	
5:00	
5:30	
6:00	
6:30	
7:00	
7:30	
8:00	
8:30	
9:00	
9:30	
10:00	
10:30	
11:00	
11:30	
12:00	
12:30	

STEP IT UP
SATURDAY ☐
TODAY'S GOAL

Time	
5:00	
5:30	
6:00	
6:30	
7:00	
7:30	
8:00	
8:30	
9:00	
9:30	
10:00	
10:30	
11:00	
11:30	
12:00	
12:30	
1:00	
1:30	
2:00	
2:30	
3:00	
3:30	
4:00	
4:30	
5:00	
5:30	
6:00	
6:30	
7:00	
7:30	
8:00	
8:30	
9:00	
9:30	
10:00	
10:30	
11:00	
11:30	
12:00	
12:30	

SOULFUL
SUNDAY ☐
TODAY'S GOAL

Time	
5:00	
5:30	
6:00	
6:30	
7:00	
7:30	
8:00	
8:30	
9:00	
9:30	
10:00	
10:30	
11:00	
11:30	
12:00	
12:30	
1:00	
1:30	
2:00	
2:30	
3:00	
3:30	
4:00	
4:30	
5:00	
5:30	
6:00	
6:30	
7:00	
7:30	
8:00	
8:30	
9:00	
9:30	
10:00	
10:30	
11:00	
11:30	
12:00	
12:30	

We are what we repeatedly do... Excellence, then is NOT an act, but a HABIT!

	MON	TUES	WED	THURS	FRI	SAT	SUN
10 *BEFORE* 10 GRATITUDE							
DECLARATIONS							
AUDIO							
READ							
FITNESS							
CONTACT 5 *BY* 5							

THOUGHTS / IDEAS / VISIONS / DREAMS

THIS WEEK'S GOAL / FOCUS

WHAT DO I NEED TO...

STOP _____

_____

START _____

_____

CONTINUE _____

_____

QUOTE OF THE WEEK

"Identify your problems, but give your power and energy to solutions."
TONY ROBBINS

DECLARATION OF THE WEEK

I am worthy and deserving of love, joy, and success..

WRITE YOUR OWN DECLARATIONS FOR THIS WEEK BELOW:

_____

_____

_____

_____

_____

_____

_____

_____

_____

_____

_____

_____

_____

_____

_____

_____

MAXIMIZE YOUR LIFE PLANNER

MAKE IT HAPPEN MONDAY	TAKE ACTION TUESDAY	WHATEVER IT TAKES WEDNESDAY
TODAY'S GOAL	TODAY'S GOAL	TODAY'S GOAL
5:00	5:00	5:00
5:30	5:30	5:30
6:00	6:00	6:00
6:30	6:30	6:30
7:00	7:00	7:00
7:30	7:30	7:30
8:00	8:00	8:00
8:30	8:30	8:30
9:00	9:00	9:00
9:30	9:30	9:30
10:00	10:00	10:00
10:30	10:30	10:30
11:00	11:00	11:00
11:30	11:30	11:30
12:00	12:00	12:00
12:30	12:30	12:30
1:00	1:00	1:00
1:30	1:30	1:30
2:00	2:00	2:00
2:30	2:30	2:30
3:00	3:00	3:00
3:30	3:30	3:30
4:00	4:00	4:00
4:30	4:30	4:30
5:00	5:00	5:00
5:30	5:30	5:30
6:00	6:00	6:00
6:30	6:30	6:30
7:00	7:00	7:00
7:30	7:30	7:30
8:00	8:00	8:00
8:30	8:30	8:30
9:00	9:00	9:00
9:30	9:30	9:30
10:00	10:00	10:00
10:30	10:30	10:30
11:00	11:00	11:00
11:30	11:30	11:30
12:00	12:00	12:00
12:30	12:30	12:30
PERSONAL TO-DO LIST	**WORK** TO-DO LIST	**FOLLOW UP** LIST
☐	☐	/
☐	☐	/
☐	☐	/
☐	☐	/
☐	☐	/
☐	☐	/
☐	☐	/
☐	☐	/
☐	☐	/

TODAY'S GOAL	TODAY'S GOAL	TODAY'S GOAL	TODAY'S GOAL
5:00	5:00	5:00	5:00
5:30	5:30	5:30	5:30
6:00	6:00	6:00	6:00
6:30	6:30	6:30	6:30
7:00	7:00	7:00	7:00
7:30	7:30	7:30	7:30
8:00	8:00	8:00	8:00
8:30	8:30	8:30	8:30
9:00	9:00	9:00	9:00
9:30	9:30	9:30	9:30
10:00	10:00	10:00	10:00
10:30	10:30	10:30	10:30
11:00	11:00	11:00	11:00
11:30	11:30	11:30	11:30
12:00	12:00	12:00	12:00
12:30	12:30	12:30	12:30
1:00	1:00	1:00	1:00
1:30	1:30	1:30	1:30
2:00	2:00	2:00	2:00
2:30	2:30	2:30	2:30
3:00	3:00	3:00	3:00
3:30	3:30	3:30	3:30
4:00	4:00	4:00	4:00
4:30	4:30	4:30	4:30
5:00	5:00	5:00	5:00
5:30	5:30	5:30	5:30
6:00	6:00	6:00	6:00
6:30	6:30	6:30	6:30
7:00	7:00	7:00	7:00
7:30	7:30	7:30	7:30
8:00	8:00	8:00	8:00
8:30	8:30	8:30	8:30
9:00	9:00	9:00	9:00
9:30	9:30	9:30	9:30
10:00	10:00	10:00	10:00
10:30	10:30	10:30	10:30
11:00	11:00	11:00	11:00
11:30	11:30	11:30	11:30
12:00	12:00	12:00	12:00
12:30	12:30	12:30	12:30

We are what we repeatedly do... Excellence, then is NOT an act, but a HABIT!

	MON	TUES	WED	THURS	FRI	SAT	SUN
10 *BEFORE* 10 GRATITUDE							
DECLARATIONS							
AUDIO							
READ							
FITNESS							
CONTACT 5 *BY* 5							

THOUGHTS / IDEAS / VISIONS / DREAMS

WEEK OF
/ / – / /

THIS WEEK'S GOAL / FOCUS

WHAT DO I NEED TO...

STOP _____

_____

START _____

_____

CONTINUE _____

_____

QUOTE OF THE WEEK

"Develop success from failures. Discouragement and failure are two of the surest stepping stones to success."
DALE CARNEGIE

DECLARATION OF THE WEEK

I am God's Masterpiece, because I am a piece of the master.

WRITE YOUR OWN DECLARATIONS FOR THIS WEEK BELOW:

_____
_____
_____
_____
_____
_____
_____
_____
_____
_____
_____
_____
_____
_____
_____
_____
_____

MAXIMIZE YOUR LIFE PLANNER

MAKE IT HAPPEN **MONDAY** ☐	*TAKE ACTION* **TUESDAY** ☐	*WHATEVER IT TAKES* **WEDNESDAY** ☐
TODAY'S GOAL	TODAY'S GOAL	TODAY'S GOAL
5:00	5:00	5:00
5:30	5:30	5:30
6:00	6:00	6:00
6:30	6:30	6:30
7:00	7:00	7:00
7:30	7:30	7:30
8:00	8:00	8:00
8:30	8:30	8:30
9:00	9:00	9:00
9:30	9:30	9:30
10:00	10:00	10:00
10:30	10:30	10:30
11:00	11:00	11:00
11:30	11:30	11:30
12:00	12:00	12:00
12:30	12:30	12:30
1:00	1:00	1:00
1:30	1:30	1:30
2:00	2:00	2:00
2:30	2:30	2:30
3:00	3:00	3:00
3:30	3:30	3:30
4:00	4:00	4:00
4:30	4:30	4:30
5:00	5:00	5:00
5:30	5:30	5:30
6:00	6:00	6:00
6:30	6:30	6:30
7:00	7:00	7:00
7:30	7:30	7:30
8:00	8:00	8:00
8:30	8:30	8:30
9:00	9:00	9:00
9:30	9:30	9:30
10:00	10:00	10:00
10:30	10:30	10:30
11:00	11:00	11:00
11:30	11:30	11:30
12:00	12:00	12:00
12:30	12:30	12:30
PERSONAL TO-DO LIST	**WORK** TO-DO LIST	**FOLLOW UP** LIST
☐	☐	/
☐	☐	/
☐	☐	/
☐	☐	/
☐	☐	/
☐	☐	/
☐	☐	/
☐	☐	/
☐	☐	/

TODAY'S GOAL	TODAY'S GOAL	TODAY'S GOAL	TODAY'S GOAL

THURSDAY	FRIDAY	SATURDAY	SUNDAY
5:00	5:00	5:00	5:00
5:30	5:30	5:30	5:30
6:00	6:00	6:00	6:00
6:30	6:30	6:30	6:30
7:00	7:00	7:00	7:00
7:30	7:30	7:30	7:30
8:00	8:00	8:00	8:00
8:30	8:30	8:30	8:30
9:00	9:00	9:00	9:00
9:30	9:30	9:30	9:30
10:00	10:00	10:00	10:00
10:30	10:30	10:30	10:30
11:00	11:00	11:00	11:00
11:30	11:30	11:30	11:30
12:00	12:00	12:00	12:00
12:30	12:30	12:30	12:30
1:00	1:00	1:00	1:00
1:30	1:30	1:30	1:30
2:00	2:00	2:00	2:00
2:30	2:30	2:30	2:30
3:00	3:00	3:00	3:00
3:30	3:30	3:30	3:30
4:00	4:00	4:00	4:00
4:30	4:30	4:30	4:30
5:00	5:00	5:00	5:00
5:30	5:30	5:30	5:30
6:00	6:00	6:00	6:00
6:30	6:30	6:30	6:30
7:00	7:00	7:00	7:00
7:30	7:30	7:30	7:30
8:00	8:00	8:00	8:00
8:30	8:30	8:30	8:30
9:00	9:00	9:00	9:00
9:30	9:30	9:30	9:30
10:00	10:00	10:00	10:00
10:30	10:30	10:30	10:30
11:00	11:00	11:00	11:00
11:30	11:30	11:30	11:30
12:00	12:00	12:00	12:00
12:30	12:30	12:30	12:30

We are what we repeatedly do... Excellence, then is NOT an act, but a HABIT!

	MON	TUES	WED	THURS	FRI	SAT	SUN
10 *BEFORE* 10 GRATITUDE							
DECLARATIONS							
AUDIO							
READ							
FITNESS							
CONTACT 5 *BY* 5							

THOUGHTS / IDEAS / VISIONS / DREAMS

WEEK OF
/ / - / /

THIS WEEK'S GOAL / FOCUS

WHAT DO I NEED TO...

STOP _____

_____

START _____

_____

CONTINUE _____

_____

_____

QUOTE OF THE WEEK

"If you change the way you look at things, the things you look at change."
WAYNE DYER

DECLARATION OF THE WEEK

God's divine power gives me everything I need for my life.

WRITE YOUR OWN DECLARATIONS FOR THIS WEEK BELOW:

_____
_____
_____
_____
_____
_____
_____
_____
_____
_____
_____
_____
_____
_____
_____
_____
_____
_____
_____

MAXIMIZE YOUR LIFE
PLANNER

MAKE IT HAPPEN **MONDAY** ☐	*TAKE ACTION* **TUESDAY** ☐	*WHATEVER IT TAKES* **WEDNESDAY** ☐
TODAY'S GOAL	TODAY'S GOAL	TODAY'S GOAL
5:00	5:00	5:00
5:30	5:30	5:30
6:00	6:00	6:00
6:30	6:30	6:30
7:00	7:00	7:00
7:30	7:30	7:30
8:00	8:00	8:00
8:30	8:30	8:30
9:00	9:00	9:00
9:30	9:30	9:30
10:00	10:00	10:00
10:30	10:30	10:30
11:00	11:00	11:00
11:30	11:30	11:30
12:00	12:00	12:00
12:30	12:30	12:30
1:00	1:00	1:00
1:30	1:30	1:30
2:00	2:00	2:00
2:30	2:30	2:30
3:00	3:00	3:00
3:30	3:30	3:30
4:00	4:00	4:00
4:30	4:30	4:30
5:00	5:00	5:00
5:30	5:30	5:30
6:00	6:00	6:00
6:30	6:30	6:30
7:00	7:00	7:00
7:30	7:30	7:30
8:00	8:00	8:00
8:30	8:30	8:30
9:00	9:00	9:00
9:30	9:30	9:30
10:00	10:00	10:00
10:30	10:30	10:30
11:00	11:00	11:00
11:30	11:30	11:30
12:00	12:00	12:00
12:30	12:30	12:30

PERSONAL TO-DO LIST	**WORK** TO-DO LIST	**FOLLOW UP** LIST
☐	☐	/
☐	☐	/
☐	☐	/
☐	☐	/
☐	☐	/
☐	☐	/
☐	☐	/
☐	☐	/
☐	☐	/

TURN IT UP **THURSDAY** ☐	FINISH STRONG **FRIDAY** ☐	STEP IT UP **SATURDAY** ☐	SOULFUL **SUNDAY** ☐
TODAY'S GOAL	TODAY'S GOAL	TODAY'S GOAL	TODAY'S GOAL

THURSDAY	FRIDAY	SATURDAY	SUNDAY
5:00	5:00	5:00	5:00
5:30	5:30	5:30	5:30
6:00	6:00	6:00	6:00
6:30	6:30	6:30	6:30
7:00	7:00	7:00	7:00
7:30	7:30	7:30	7:30
8:00	8:00	8:00	8:00
8:30	8:30	8:30	8:30
9:00	9:00	9:00	9:00
9:30	9:30	9:30	9:30
10:00	10:00	10:00	10:00
10:30	10:30	10:30	10:30
11:00	11:00	11:00	11:00
11:30	11:30	11:30	11:30
12:00	12:00	12:00	12:00
12:30	12:30	12:30	12:30
1:00	1:00	1:00	1:00
1:30	1:30	1:30	1:30
2:00	2:00	2:00	2:00
2:30	2:30	2:30	2:30
3:00	3:00	3:00	3:00
3:30	3:30	3:30	3:30
4:00	4:00	4:00	4:00
4:30	4:30	4:30	4:30
5:00	5:00	5:00	5:00
5:30	5:30	5:30	5:30
6:00	6:00	6:00	6:00
6:30	6:30	6:30	6:30
7:00	7:00	7:00	7:00
7:30	7:30	7:30	7:30
8:00	8:00	8:00	8:00
8:30	8:30	8:30	8:30
9:00	9:00	9:00	9:00
9:30	9:30	9:30	9:30
10:00	10:00	10:00	10:00
10:30	10:30	10:30	10:30
11:00	11:00	11:00	11:00
11:30	11:30	11:30	11:30
12:00	12:00	12:00	12:00
12:30	12:30	12:30	12:30

We are what we repeatedly do... Excellence, then is NOT an act, but a HABIT!	MON	TUES	WED	THURS	FRI	SAT	SUN
10 *BEFORE* 10 GRATITUDE							
DECLARATIONS							
AUDIO							
READ							
FITNESS							
CONTACT 5 *BY* 5							

THOUGHTS / IDEAS / VISIONS / DREAMS

WEEK OF
/ / - / /

THIS WEEK'S GOAL / FOCUS

WHAT DO I NEED TO...

STOP _____

_____

START _____

_____

CONTINUE _____

_____

QUOTE OF THE WEEK

"The price of success is hard work, dedication to the job at hand, and the determination that whether we win or lose, we have applied the best of ourselves to the task at hand."

VINCE LOMBARDI

DECLARATION OF THE WEEK

I am so happy and grateful now that money comes to me in increasing quantities through multiple sources on a continuous basis.

WRITE YOUR OWN DECLARATIONS FOR THIS WEEK BELOW:

_____
_____
_____
_____
_____
_____
_____
_____
_____
_____

MAXIMIZE YOUR LIFE
PLANNER

MAKE IT HAPPEN MONDAY ☐	*TAKE ACTION* TUESDAY ☐	*WHATEVER IT TAKES* WEDNESDAY ☐
TODAY'S GOAL	TODAY'S GOAL	TODAY'S GOAL
5:00	5:00	5:00
5:30	5:30	5:30
6:00	6:00	6:00
6:30	6:30	6:30
7:00	7:00	7:00
7:30	7:30	7:30
8:00	8:00	8:00
8:30	8:30	8:30
9:00	9:00	9:00
9:30	9:30	9:30
10:00	10:00	10:00
10:30	10:30	10:30
11:00	11:00	11:00
11:30	11:30	11:30
12:00	12:00	12:00
12:30	12:30	12:30
1:00	1:00	1:00
1:30	1:30	1:30
2:00	2:00	2:00
2:30	2:30	2:30
3:00	3:00	3:00
3:30	3:30	3:30
4:00	4:00	4:00
4:30	4:30	4:30
5:00	5:00	5:00
5:30	5:30	5:30
6:00	6:00	6:00
6:30	6:30	6:30
7:00	7:00	7:00
7:30	7:30	7:30
8:00	8:00	8:00
8:30	8:30	8:30
9:00	9:00	9:00
9:30	9:30	9:30
10:00	10:00	10:00
10:30	10:30	10:30
11:00	11:00	11:00
11:30	11:30	11:30
12:00	12:00	12:00
12:30	12:30	12:30

PERSONAL TO-DO LIST	**WORK** TO-DO LIST	**FOLLOW UP** LIST
☐	☐	/
☐	☐	/
☐	☐	/
☐	☐	/
☐	☐	/
☐	☐	/
☐	☐	/
☐	☐	/
☐	☐	/

	TURN IT UP			FINISH STRONG			STEP IT UP			SOULFUL	
	THURSDAY	☐		**FRIDAY**	☐		**SATURDAY**	☐		**SUNDAY**	☐

TODAY'S GOAL		TODAY'S GOAL		TODAY'S GOAL		TODAY'S GOAL	
5:00		5:00		5:00		5:00	
5:30		5:30		5:30		5:30	
6:00		6:00		6:00		6:00	
6:30		6:30		6:30		6:30	
7:00		7:00		7:00		7:00	
7:30		7:30		7:30		7:30	
8:00		8:00		8:00		8:00	
8:30		8:30		8:30		8:30	
9:00		9:00		9:00		9:00	
9:30		9:30		9:30		9:30	
10:00		10:00		10:00		10:00	
10:30		10:30		10:30		10:30	
11:00		11:00		11:00		11:00	
11:30		11:30		11:30		11:30	
12:00		12:00		12:00		12:00	
12:30		12:30		12:30		12:30	
1:00		1:00		1:00		1:00	
1:30		1:30		1:30		1:30	
2:00		2:00		2:00		2:00	
2:30		2:30		2:30		2:30	
3:00		3:00		3:00		3:00	
3:30		3:30		3:30		3:30	
4:00		4:00		4:00		4:00	
4:30		4:30		4:30		4:30	
5:00		5:00		5:00		5:00	
5:30		5:30		5:30		5:30	
6:00		6:00		6:00		6:00	
6:30		6:30		6:30		6:30	
7:00		7:00		7:00		7:00	
7:30		7:30		7:30		7:30	
8:00		8:00		8:00		8:00	
8:30		8:30		8:30		8:30	
9:00		9:00		9:00		9:00	
9:30		9:30		9:30		9:30	
10:00		10:00		10:00		10:00	
10:30		10:30		10:30		10:30	
11:00		11:00		11:00		11:00	
11:30		11:30		11:30		11:30	
12:00		12:00		12:00		12:00	
12:30		12:30		12:30		12:30	

We are what we repeatedly do... Excellence, then is NOT an act, but a HABIT!	MON	TUES	WED	THURS	FRI	SAT	SUN
10 BEFORE 10 GRATITUDE							
DECLARATIONS							
AUDIO							
READ							
FITNESS							
CONTACT 5 BY 5							

THOUGHTS / IDEAS / VISIONS / DREAMS

THIS WEEK'S GOAL / FOCUS

WHAT DO I NEED TO...

STOP _____
_____
_____

START _____
_____
_____

CONTINUE _____
_____
_____

QUOTE OF THE WEEK

"Be faithful in small things because it is in them that your strength lies."
MOTHER TERESA

DECLARATION OF THE WEEK

I am an amazing leader, and creator of leaders.

WRITE YOUR OWN DECLARATIONS FOR THIS WEEK BELOW:

_____
_____
_____
_____
_____
_____
_____
_____
_____
_____
_____
_____
_____
_____
_____
_____

MAXIMIZE YOUR LIFE PLANNER

MAKE IT HAPPEN MONDAY	*TAKE ACTION* TUESDAY	*WHATEVER IT TAKES* WEDNESDAY
TODAY'S GOAL	TODAY'S GOAL	TODAY'S GOAL
5:00	5:00	5:00
5:30	5:30	5:30
6:00	6:00	6:00
6:30	6:30	6:30
7:00	7:00	7:00
7:30	7:30	7:30
8:00	8:00	8:00
8:30	8:30	8:30
9:00	9:00	9:00
9:30	9:30	9:30
10:00	10:00	10:00
10:30	10:30	10:30
11:00	11:00	11:00
11:30	11:30	11:30
12:00	12:00	12:00
12:30	12:30	12:30
1:00	1:00	1:00
1:30	1:30	1:30
2:00	2:00	2:00
2:30	2:30	2:30
3:00	3:00	3:00
3:30	3:30	3:30
4:00	4:00	4:00
4:30	4:30	4:30
5:00	5:00	5:00
5:30	5:30	5:30
6:00	6:00	6:00
6:30	6:30	6:30
7:00	7:00	7:00
7:30	7:30	7:30
8:00	8:00	8:00
8:30	8:30	8:30
9:00	9:00	9:00
9:30	9:30	9:30
10:00	10:00	10:00
10:30	10:30	10:30
11:00	11:00	11:00
11:30	11:30	11:30
12:00	12:00	12:00
12:30	12:30	12:30
PERSONAL TO-DO LIST	**WORK** TO-DO LIST	**FOLLOW UP** LIST
☐	☐	/
☐	☐	/
☐	☐	/
☐	☐	/
☐	☐	/
☐	☐	/
☐	☐	/
☐	☐	/
☐	☐	/

TURN IT UP THURSDAY ☐	FINISH STRONG FRIDAY ☐	STEP IT UP SATURDAY ☐	SOULFUL SUNDAY ☐
TODAY'S GOAL	TODAY'S GOAL	TODAY'S GOAL	TODAY'S GOAL
5:00	5:00	5:00	5:00
5:30	5:30	5:30	5:30
6:00	6:00	6:00	6:00
6:30	6:30	6:30	6:30
7:00	7:00	7:00	7:00
7:30	7:30	7:30	7:30
8:00	8:00	8:00	8:00
8:30	8:30	8:30	8:30
9:00	9:00	9:00	9:00
9:30	9:30	9:30	9:30
10:00	10:00	10:00	10:00
10:30	10:30	10:30	10:30
11:00	11:00	11:00	11:00
11:30	11:30	11:30	11:30
12:00	12:00	12:00	12:00
12:30	12:30	12:30	12:30
1:00	1:00	1:00	1:00
1:30	1:30	1:30	1:30
2:00	2:00	2:00	2:00
2:30	2:30	2:30	2:30
3:00	3:00	3:00	3:00
3:30	3:30	3:30	3:30
4:00	4:00	4:00	4:00
4:30	4:30	4:30	4:30
5:00	5:00	5:00	5:00
5:30	5:30	5:30	5:30
6:00	6:00	6:00	6:00
6:30	6:30	6:30	6:30
7:00	7:00	7:00	7:00
7:30	7:30	7:30	7:30
8:00	8:00	8:00	8:00
8:30	8:30	8:30	8:30
9:00	9:00	9:00	9:00
9:30	9:30	9:30	9:30
10:00	10:00	10:00	10:00
10:30	10:30	10:30	10:30
11:00	11:00	11:00	11:00
11:30	11:30	11:30	11:30
12:00	12:00	12:00	12:00
12:30	12:30	12:30	12:30

We are what we repeatedly do... Excellence, then is NOT an act, but a HABIT!	MON	TUES	WED	THURS	FRI	SAT	SUN
10 *BEFORE* 10 GRATITUDE							
DECLARATIONS							
AUDIO							
READ							
FITNESS							
CONTACT 5 *BY* 5							

THOUGHTS / IDEAS / VISIONS / DREAMS

THIS WEEK'S GOAL / FOCUS

WHAT DO I NEED TO...

STOP _____

_____

START _____

_____

CONTINUE _____

_____

QUOTE OF THE WEEK

"God will meet you where you are in order to take you where He wants you to go."
TONY EVANS

DECLARATION OF THE WEEK

I am significant and contribute to the advancement of humankind.

WRITE YOUR OWN DECLARATIONS FOR THIS WEEK BELOW:

_____
_____
_____
_____
_____
_____
_____
_____
_____
_____
_____
_____
_____
_____
_____

MAXIMIZE
YOUR LIFE
PLANNER

MAKE IT HAPPEN **MONDAY** ☐	*TAKE ACTION* **TUESDAY** ☐	*WHATEVER IT TAKES* **WEDNESDAY** ☐
TODAY'S GOAL	TODAY'S GOAL	TODAY'S GOAL
5:00	5:00	5:00
5:30	5:30	5:30
6:00	6:00	6:00
6:30	6:30	6:30
7:00	7:00	7:00
7:30	7:30	7:30
8:00	8:00	8:00
8:30	8:30	8:30
9:00	9:00	9:00
9:30	9:30	9:30
10:00	10:00	10:00
10:30	10:30	10:30
11:00	11:00	11:00
11:30	11:30	11:30
12:00	12:00	12:00
12:30	12:30	12:30
1:00	1:00	1:00
1:30	1:30	1:30
2:00	2:00	2:00
2:30	2:30	2:30
3:00	3:00	3:00
3:30	3:30	3:30
4:00	4:00	4:00
4:30	4:30	4:30
5:00	5:00	5:00
5:30	5:30	5:30
6:00	6:00	6:00
6:30	6:30	6:30
7:00	7:00	7:00
7:30	7:30	7:30
8:00	8:00	8:00
8:30	8:30	8:30
9:00	9:00	9:00
9:30	9:30	9:30
10:00	10:00	10:00
10:30	10:30	10:30
11:00	11:00	11:00
11:30	11:30	11:30
12:00	12:00	12:00
12:30	12:30	12:30
PERSONAL TO-DO LIST	**WORK** TO-DO LIST	**FOLLOW UP** LIST
☐	☐	/
☐	☐	/
☐	☐	/
☐	☐	/
☐	☐	/
☐	☐	/
☐	☐	/
☐	☐	/
☐	☐	/
☐	☐	/

TURN IT UP		FINISH STRONG		STEP IT UP		SOULFUL	
THURSDAY	☐	**FRIDAY**	☐	**SATURDAY**	☐	**SUNDAY**	☐

TODAY'S GOAL	TODAY'S GOAL	TODAY'S GOAL	TODAY'S GOAL

THURSDAY		FRIDAY		SATURDAY		SUNDAY	
5:00		5:00		5:00		5:00	
5:30		5:30		5:30		5:30	
6:00		6:00		6:00		6:00	
6:30		6:30		6:30		6:30	
7:00		7:00		7:00		7:00	
7:30		7:30		7:30		7:30	
8:00		8:00		8:00		8:00	
8:30		8:30		8:30		8:30	
9:00		9:00		9:00		9:00	
9:30		9:30		9:30		9:30	
10:00		10:00		10:00		10:00	
10:30		10:30		10:30		10:30	
11:00		11:00		11:00		11:00	
11:30		11:30		11:30		11:30	
12:00		12:00		12:00		12:00	
12:30		12:30		12:30		12:30	
1:00		1:00		1:00		1:00	
1:30		1:30		1:30		1:30	
2:00		2:00		2:00		2:00	
2:30		2:30		2:30		2:30	
3:00		3:00		3:00		3:00	
3:30		3:30		3:30		3:30	
4:00		4:00		4:00		4:00	
4:30		4:30		4:30		4:30	
5:00		5:00		5:00		5:00	
5:30		5:30		5:30		5:30	
6:00		6:00		6:00		6:00	
6:30		6:30		6:30		6:30	
7:00		7:00		7:00		7:00	
7:30		7:30		7:30		7:30	
8:00		8:00		8:00		8:00	
8:30		8:30		8:30		8:30	
9:00		9:00		9:00		9:00	
9:30		9:30		9:30		9:30	
10:00		10:00		10:00		10:00	
10:30		10:30		10:30		10:30	
11:00		11:00		11:00		11:00	
11:30		11:30		11:30		11:30	
12:00		12:00		12:00		12:00	
12:30		12:30		12:30		12:30	

We are what we repeatedly do... Excellence, then is NOT an act, but a HABIT!	MON	TUES	WED	THURS	FRI	SAT	SUN
10 *BEFORE* **10 GRATITUDE**							
DECLARATIONS							
AUDIO							
READ							
FITNESS							
CONTACT 5 *BY* **5**							

THOUGHTS / IDEAS / VISIONS / DREAMS

WEEK OF
/ / - / /

THIS WEEK'S GOAL / FOCUS

WHAT DO I NEED TO...

STOP _____

_____

START _____

_____

CONTINUE _____

_____

QUOTE OF THE WEEK

*"If you can't fly, then run...
If you can't run, then walk...
If you can't walk, then crawl...
but whatever you do, you have
to keep moving forward.."*
MARTIN LUTHER KING JR.

DECLARATION OF THE WEEK

*I give out love in all my
relationships, and it is
returned to me ten fold.*

WRITE YOUR OWN DECLARATIONS FOR THIS WEEK BELOW:

_____
_____
_____
_____
_____
_____
_____
_____
_____
_____
_____
_____
_____
_____

MAXIMIZE YOUR LIFE PLANNER

MAKE IT HAPPEN **MONDAY**	*TAKE ACTION* **TUESDAY**	*WHATEVER IT TAKES* **WEDNESDAY**
TODAY'S GOAL	TODAY'S GOAL	TODAY'S GOAL
5:00	5:00	5:00
5:30	5:30	5:30
6:00	6:00	6:00
6:30	6:30	6:30
7:00	7:00	7:00
7:30	7:30	7:30
8:00	8:00	8:00
8:30	8:30	8:30
9:00	9:00	9:00
9:30	9:30	9:30
10:00	10:00	10:00
10:30	10:30	10:30
11:00	11:00	11:00
11:30	11:30	11:30
12:00	12:00	12:00
12:30	12:30	12:30
1:00	1:00	1:00
1:30	1:30	1:30
2:00	2:00	2:00
2:30	2:30	2:30
3:00	3:00	3:00
3:30	3:30	3:30
4:00	4:00	4:00
4:30	4:30	4:30
5:00	5:00	5:00
5:30	5:30	5:30
6:00	6:00	6:00
6:30	6:30	6:30
7:00	7:00	7:00
7:30	7:30	7:30
8:00	8:00	8:00
8:30	8:30	8:30
9:00	9:00	9:00
9:30	9:30	9:30
10:00	10:00	10:00
10:30	10:30	10:30
11:00	11:00	11:00
11:30	11:30	11:30
12:00	12:00	12:00
12:30	12:30	12:30
PERSONAL TO-DO LIST	**WORK** TO-DO LIST	**FOLLOW UP** LIST
☐	☐	/
☐	☐	/
☐	☐	/
☐	☐	/
☐	☐	/
☐	☐	/
☐	☐	/
☐	☐	/
☐	☐	/

TODAY'S GOAL	TODAY'S GOAL	TODAY'S GOAL	TODAY'S GOAL

THURSDAY	FRIDAY	SATURDAY	SUNDAY
5:00	5:00	5:00	5:00
5:30	5:30	5:30	5:30
6:00	6:00	6:00	6:00
6:30	6:30	6:30	6:30
7:00	7:00	7:00	7:00
7:30	7:30	7:30	7:30
8:00	8:00	8:00	8:00
8:30	8:30	8:30	8:30
9:00	9:00	9:00	9:00
9:30	9:30	9:30	9:30
10:00	10:00	10:00	10:00
10:30	10:30	10:30	10:30
11:00	11:00	11:00	11:00
11:30	11:30	11:30	11:30
12:00	12:00	12:00	12:00
12:30	12:30	12:30	12:30
1:00	1:00	1:00	1:00
1:30	1:30	1:30	1:30
2:00	2:00	2:00	2:00
2:30	2:30	2:30	2:30
3:00	3:00	3:00	3:00
3:30	3:30	3:30	3:30
4:00	4:00	4:00	4:00
4:30	4:30	4:30	4:30
5:00	5:00	5:00	5:00
5:30	5:30	5:30	5:30
6:00	6:00	6:00	6:00
6:30	6:30	6:30	6:30
7:00	7:00	7:00	7:00
7:30	7:30	7:30	7:30
8:00	8:00	8:00	8:00
8:30	8:30	8:30	8:30
9:00	9:00	9:00	9:00
9:30	9:30	9:30	9:30
10:00	10:00	10:00	10:00
10:30	10:30	10:30	10:30
11:00	11:00	11:00	11:00
11:30	11:30	11:30	11:30
12:00	12:00	12:00	12:00
12:30	12:30	12:30	12:30

We are what we repeatedly do... Excellence, then is NOT an act, but a HABIT!	MON	TUES	WED	THURS	FRI	SAT	SUN
10 *BEFORE* **10 GRATITUDE**							
DECLARATIONS							
AUDIO							
READ							
FITNESS							
CONTACT 5 *BY* **5**							

THOUGHTS / IDEAS / VISIONS / DREAMS

WEEK OF
/ / - / /

THIS WEEK'S GOAL / FOCUS

WHAT DO I NEED TO...

STOP _____
_____

START _____
_____

CONTINUE _____
_____

QUOTE OF THE WEEK

"The best and most beautiful things in the world cannot be seen or even touched. They must be felt with the heart."
HELEN KELLER

DECLARATION OF THE WEEK

I am healthy, wealthy, and wise.

WRITE YOUR OWN DECLARATIONS FOR THIS WEEK BELOW:

_____
_____
_____
_____
_____
_____
_____
_____
_____
_____
_____
_____
_____
_____
_____
_____
_____
_____

MAXIMIZE YOUR LIFE PLANNER

MAKE IT HAPPEN MONDAY ☐	*TAKE ACTION* TUESDAY ☐	*WHATEVER IT TAKES* WEDNESDAY ☐
TODAY'S GOAL	TODAY'S GOAL	TODAY'S GOAL
5:00	5:00	5:00
5:30	5:30	5:30
6:00	6:00	6:00
6:30	6:30	6:30
7:00	7:00	7:00
7:30	7:30	7:30
8:00	8:00	8:00
8:30	8:30	8:30
9:00	9:00	9:00
9:30	9:30	9:30
10:00	10:00	10:00
10:30	10:30	10:30
11:00	11:00	11:00
11:30	11:30	11:30
12:00	12:00	12:00
12:30	12:30	12:30
1:00	1:00	1:00
1:30	1:30	1:30
2:00	2:00	2:00
2:30	2:30	2:30
3:00	3:00	3:00
3:30	3:30	3:30
4:00	4:00	4:00
4:30	4:30	4:30
5:00	5:00	5:00
5:30	5:30	5:30
6:00	6:00	6:00
6:30	6:30	6:30
7:00	7:00	7:00
7:30	7:30	7:30
8:00	8:00	8:00
8:30	8:30	8:30
9:00	9:00	9:00
9:30	9:30	9:30
10:00	10:00	10:00
10:30	10:30	10:30
11:00	11:00	11:00
11:30	11:30	11:30
12:00	12:00	12:00
12:30	12:30	12:30
PERSONAL TO-DO LIST	**WORK** TO-DO LIST	**FOLLOW UP** LIST
☐	☐	/
☐	☐	/
☐	☐	/
☐	☐	/
☐	☐	/
☐	☐	/
☐	☐	/
☐	☐	/
☐	☐	/

TURN IT UP   ☐
THURSDAY

FINISH STRONG   ☐
FRIDAY

STEP IT UP   ☐
SATURDAY

SOULFUL   ☐
SUNDAY

THURSDAY TODAY'S GOAL	FRIDAY TODAY'S GOAL	SATURDAY TODAY'S GOAL	SUNDAY TODAY'S GOAL
5:00	5:00	5:00	5:00
5:30	5:30	5:30	5:30
6:00	6:00	6:00	6:00
6:30	6:30	6:30	6:30
7:00	7:00	7:00	7:00
7:30	7:30	7:30	7:30
8:00	8:00	8:00	8:00
8:30	8:30	8:30	8:30
9:00	9:00	9:00	9:00
9:30	9:30	9:30	9:30
10:00	10:00	10:00	10:00
10:30	10:30	10:30	10:30
11:00	11:00	11:00	11:00
11:30	11:30	11:30	11:30
12:00	12:00	12:00	12:00
12:30	12:30	12:30	12:30
1:00	1:00	1:00	1:00
1:30	1:30	1:30	1:30
2:00	2:00	2:00	2:00
2:30	2:30	2:30	2:30
3:00	3:00	3:00	3:00
3:30	3:30	3:30	3:30
4:00	4:00	4:00	4:00
4:30	4:30	4:30	4:30
5:00	5:00	5:00	5:00
5:30	5:30	5:30	5:30
6:00	6:00	6:00	6:00
6:30	6:30	6:30	6:30
7:00	7:00	7:00	7:00
7:30	7:30	7:30	7:30
8:00	8:00	8:00	8:00
8:30	8:30	8:30	8:30
9:00	9:00	9:00	9:00
9:30	9:30	9:30	9:30
10:00	10:00	10:00	10:00
10:30	10:30	10:30	10:30
11:00	11:00	11:00	11:00
11:30	11:30	11:30	11:30
12:00	12:00	12:00	12:00
12:30	12:30	12:30	12:30

We are what we repeatedly do... Excellence, then is NOT an act, but a HABIT!	MON	TUES	WED	THURS	FRI	SAT	SUN
10 *BEFORE* 10 GRATITUDE							
DECLARATIONS							
AUDIO							
READ							
FITNESS							
CONTACT 5 *BY* 5							

THOUGHTS / IDEAS / VISIONS / DREAMS

THIS WEEK'S GOAL / FOCUS

WHAT DO I NEED TO...

STOP _____
_____

START _____
_____

CONTINUE _____
_____

QUOTE OF THE WEEK

"Never give up on a dream just because of the time it will take to accomplish it. The time will pass anyway."
EARL NIGHTINGALE

DECLARATION OF THE WEEK

I am open to an even better outcome than the one I desire.

WRITE YOUR OWN DECLARATIONS FOR THIS WEEK BELOW:

_____
_____
_____
_____
_____
_____
_____
_____
_____
_____
_____
_____
_____
_____
_____
_____

MAXIMIZE YOUR LIFE PLANNER

MAKE IT HAPPEN MONDAY ☐	*TAKE ACTION* TUESDAY ☐	*WHATEVER IT TAKES* WEDNESDAY ☐
TODAY'S GOAL	TODAY'S GOAL	TODAY'S GOAL
5:00	5:00	5:00
5:30	5:30	5:30
6:00	6:00	6:00
6:30	6:30	6:30
7:00	7:00	7:00
7:30	7:30	7:30
8:00	8:00	8:00
8:30	8:30	8:30
9:00	9:00	9:00
9:30	9:30	9:30
10:00	10:00	10:00
10:30	10:30	10:30
11:00	11:00	11:00
11:30	11:30	11:30
12:00	12:00	12:00
12:30	12:30	12:30
1:00	1:00	1:00
1:30	1:30	1:30
2:00	2:00	2:00
2:30	2:30	2:30
3:00	3:00	3:00
3:30	3:30	3:30
4:00	4:00	4:00
4:30	4:30	4:30
5:00	5:00	5:00
5:30	5:30	5:30
6:00	6:00	6:00
6:30	6:30	6:30
7:00	7:00	7:00
7:30	7:30	7:30
8:00	8:00	8:00
8:30	8:30	8:30
9:00	9:00	9:00
9:30	9:30	9:30
10:00	10:00	10:00
10:30	10:30	10:30
11:00	11:00	11:00
11:30	11:30	11:30
12:00	12:00	12:00
12:30	12:30	12:30
PERSONAL TO-DO LIST	**WORK** TO-DO LIST	**FOLLOW UP** LIST
☐	☐	/
☐	☐	/
☐	☐	/
☐	☐	/
☐	☐	/
☐	☐	/
☐	☐	/
☐	☐	/
☐	☐	/

TURN IT UP
THURSDAY

FINISH STRONG
FRIDAY

STEP IT UP
SATURDAY

SOULFUL
SUNDAY

TODAY'S GOAL (THURSDAY)	TODAY'S GOAL (FRIDAY)	TODAY'S GOAL (SATURDAY)	TODAY'S GOAL (SUNDAY)
5:00	5:00	5:00	5:00
5:30	5:30	5:30	5:30
6:00	6:00	6:00	6:00
6:30	6:30	6:30	6:30
7:00	7:00	7:00	7:00
7:30	7:30	7:30	7:30
8:00	8:00	8:00	8:00
8:30	8:30	8:30	8:30
9:00	9:00	9:00	9:00
9:30	9:30	9:30	9:30
10:00	10:00	10:00	10:00
10:30	10:30	10:30	10:30
11:00	11:00	11:00	11:00
11:30	11:30	11:30	11:30
12:00	12:00	12:00	12:00
12:30	12:30	12:30	12:30
1:00	1:00	1:00	1:00
1:30	1:30	1:30	1:30
2:00	2:00	2:00	2:00
2:30	2:30	2:30	2:30
3:00	3:00	3:00	3:00
3:30	3:30	3:30	3:30
4:00	4:00	4:00	4:00
4:30	4:30	4:30	4:30
5:00	5:00	5:00	5:00
5:30	5:30	5:30	5:30
6:00	6:00	6:00	6:00
6:30	6:30	6:30	6:30
7:00	7:00	7:00	7:00
7:30	7:30	7:30	7:30
8:00	8:00	8:00	8:00
8:30	8:30	8:30	8:30
9:00	9:00	9:00	9:00
9:30	9:30	9:30	9:30
10:00	10:00	10:00	10:00
10:30	10:30	10:30	10:30
11:00	11:00	11:00	11:00
11:30	11:30	11:30	11:30
12:00	12:00	12:00	12:00
12:30	12:30	12:30	12:30

We are what we repeatedly do... Excellence, then is NOT an act, but a HABIT!

	MON	TUES	WED	THURS	FRI	SAT	SUN
10 *BEFORE* **10 GRATITUDE**							
DECLARATIONS							
AUDIO							
READ							
FITNESS							
CONTACT 5 *BY* **5**							

THOUGHTS / IDEAS / VISIONS / DREAMS

WEEK OF
/ / - / /

THIS WEEK'S GOAL / FOCUS

WHAT DO I NEED TO...

STOP _____
_____
_____

START _____
_____
_____

CONTINUE _____
_____
_____

QUOTE OF THE WEEK
"Too many of us are not living our dreams because we are living our fears."
LES BROWN

DECLARATION OF THE WEEK
My thoughts are filled with positivity, and my life is full with prosperity..

WRITE YOUR OWN DECLARATIONS FOR THIS WEEK BELOW:
_____
_____
_____
_____
_____
_____
_____
_____
_____
_____
_____
_____
_____
_____
_____
_____
_____

MAXIMIZE
YOUR LIFE
PLANNER

MAKE IT HAPPEN **MONDAY** ☐	*TAKE ACTION* **TUESDAY** ☐	*WHATEVER IT TAKES* **WEDNESDAY** ☐
TODAY'S GOAL	TODAY'S GOAL	TODAY'S GOAL
5:00	5:00	5:00
5:30	5:30	5:30
6:00	6:00	6:00
6:30	6:30	6:30
7:00	7:00	7:00
7:30	7:30	7:30
8:00	8:00	8:00
8:30	8:30	8:30
9:00	9:00	9:00
9:30	9:30	9:30
10:00	10:00	10:00
10:30	10:30	10:30
11:00	11:00	11:00
11:30	11:30	11:30
12:00	12:00	12:00
12:30	12:30	12:30
1:00	1:00	1:00
1:30	1:30	1:30
2:00	2:00	2:00
2:30	2:30	2:30
3:00	3:00	3:00
3:30	3:30	3:30
4:00	4:00	4:00
4:30	4:30	4:30
5:00	5:00	5:00
5:30	5:30	5:30
6:00	6:00	6:00
6:30	6:30	6:30
7:00	7:00	7:00
7:30	7:30	7:30
8:00	8:00	8:00
8:30	8:30	8:30
9:00	9:00	9:00
9:30	9:30	9:30
10:00	10:00	10:00
10:30	10:30	10:30
11:00	11:00	11:00
11:30	11:30	11:30
12:00	12:00	12:00
12:30	12:30	12:30
PERSONAL TO-DO LIST	**WORK** TO-DO LIST	**FOLLOW UP** LIST
☐	☐	/
☐	☐	/
☐	☐	/
☐	☐	/
☐	☐	/
☐	☐	/
☐	☐	/
☐	☐	/
☐	☐	/

TURN IT UP THURSDAY		FINISH STRONG FRIDAY		STEP IT UP SATURDAY		SOULFUL SUNDAY	
TODAY'S GOAL		**TODAY'S GOAL**		**TODAY'S GOAL**		**TODAY'S GOAL**	

THURSDAY		FRIDAY		SATURDAY		SUNDAY	
5:00		5:00		5:00		5:00	
5:30		5:30		5:30		5:30	
6:00		6:00		6:00		6:00	
6:30		6:30		6:30		6:30	
7:00		7:00		7:00		7:00	
7:30		7:30		7:30		7:30	
8:00		8:00		8:00		8:00	
8:30		8:30		8:30		8:30	
9:00		9:00		9:00		9:00	
9:30		9:30		9:30		9:30	
10:00		10:00		10:00		10:00	
10:30		10:30		10:30		10:30	
11:00		11:00		11:00		11:00	
11:30		11:30		11:30		11:30	
12:00		12:00		12:00		12:00	
12:30		12:30		12:30		12:30	
1:00		1:00		1:00		1:00	
1:30		1:30		1:30		1:30	
2:00		2:00		2:00		2:00	
2:30		2:30		2:30		2:30	
3:00		3:00		3:00		3:00	
3:30		3:30		3:30		3:30	
4:00		4:00		4:00		4:00	
4:30		4:30		4:30		4:30	
5:00		5:00		5:00		5:00	
5:30		5:30		5:30		5:30	
6:00		6:00		6:00		6:00	
6:30		6:30		6:30		6:30	
7:00		7:00		7:00		7:00	
7:30		7:30		7:30		7:30	
8:00		8:00		8:00		8:00	
8:30		8:30		8:30		8:30	
9:00		9:00		9:00		9:00	
9:30		9:30		9:30		9:30	
10:00		10:00		10:00		10:00	
10:30		10:30		10:30		10:30	
11:00		11:00		11:00		11:00	
11:30		11:30		11:30		11:30	
12:00		12:00		12:00		12:00	
12:30		12:30		12:30		12:30	

We are what we repeatedly do... Excellence, then is NOT an act, but a HABIT!	MON	TUES	WED	THURS	FRI	SAT	SUN
10 *BEFORE* 10 GRATITUDE							
DECLARATIONS							
AUDIO							
READ							
FITNESS							
CONTACT 5 *BY* 5							

THOUGHTS / IDEAS / VISIONS / DREAMS

WEEK OF
/ / - / /

THIS WEEK'S GOAL / FOCUS

WHAT DO I NEED TO...

STOP _____

_____

START _____

_____

CONTINUE _____

_____

QUOTE OF THE WEEK

"The pain you feel today is the strength you feel tomorrow. For every challenge encountered there is opportunity for growth."

UNKNOWN

DECLARATION OF THE WEEK

Today is a day of completion. I give thanks for this perfect day. Miracle shall follow miracle, and wonders shall never cease.

WRITE YOUR OWN DECLARATIONS FOR THIS WEEK BELOW:

_____
_____
_____
_____
_____
_____
_____
_____
_____
_____
_____
_____
_____

MAXIMIZE YOUR LIFE
P L A N N E R

MAKE IT HAPPEN MONDAY	*TAKE ACTION* TUESDAY	*WHATEVER IT TAKES* WEDNESDAY
TODAY'S GOAL	TODAY'S GOAL	TODAY'S GOAL
5:00	5:00	5:00
5:30	5:30	5:30
6:00	6:00	6:00
6:30	6:30	6:30
7:00	7:00	7:00
7:30	7:30	7:30
8:00	8:00	8:00
8:30	8:30	8:30
9:00	9:00	9:00
9:30	9:30	9:30
10:00	10:00	10:00
10:30	10:30	10:30
11:00	11:00	11:00
11:30	11:30	11:30
12:00	12:00	12:00
12:30	12:30	12:30
1:00	1:00	1:00
1:30	1:30	1:30
2:00	2:00	2:00
2:30	2:30	2:30
3:00	3:00	3:00
3:30	3:30	3:30
4:00	4:00	4:00
4:30	4:30	4:30
5:00	5:00	5:00
5:30	5:30	5:30
6:00	6:00	6:00
6:30	6:30	6:30
7:00	7:00	7:00
7:30	7:30	7:30
8:00	8:00	8:00
8:30	8:30	8:30
9:00	9:00	9:00
9:30	9:30	9:30
10:00	10:00	10:00
10:30	10:30	10:30
11:00	11:00	11:00
11:30	11:30	11:30
12:00	12:00	12:00
12:30	12:30	12:30

PERSONAL TO-DO LIST	WORK TO-DO LIST	FOLLOW UP LIST
☐	☐	/
☐	☐	/
☐	☐	/
☐	☐	/
☐	☐	/
☐	☐	/
☐	☐	/
☐	☐	/
☐	☐	

THURSDAY TODAY'S GOAL	FRIDAY TODAY'S GOAL	SATURDAY TODAY'S GOAL	SUNDAY TODAY'S GOAL
5:00	5:00	5:00	5:00
5:30	5:30	5:30	5:30
6:00	6:00	6:00	6:00
6:30	6:30	6:30	6:30
7:00	7:00	7:00	7:00
7:30	7:30	7:30	7:30
8:00	8:00	8:00	8:00
8:30	8:30	8:30	8:30
9:00	9:00	9:00	9:00
9:30	9:30	9:30	9:30
10:00	10:00	10:00	10:00
10:30	10:30	10:30	10:30
11:00	11:00	11:00	11:00
11:30	11:30	11:30	11:30
12:00	12:00	12:00	12:00
12:30	12:30	12:30	12:30
1:00	1:00	1:00	1:00
1:30	1:30	1:30	1:30
2:00	2:00	2:00	2:00
2:30	2:30	2:30	2:30
3:00	3:00	3:00	3:00
3:30	3:30	3:30	3:30
4:00	4:00	4:00	4:00
4:30	4:30	4:30	4:30
5:00	5:00	5:00	5:00
5:30	5:30	5:30	5:30
6:00	6:00	6:00	6:00
6:30	6:30	6:30	6:30
7:00	7:00	7:00	7:00
7:30	7:30	7:30	7:30
8:00	8:00	8:00	8:00
8:30	8:30	8:30	8:30
9:00	9:00	9:00	9:00
9:30	9:30	9:30	9:30
10:00	10:00	10:00	10:00
10:30	10:30	10:30	10:30
11:00	11:00	11:00	11:00
11:30	11:30	11:30	11:30
12:00	12:00	12:00	12:00
12:30	12:30	12:30	12:30

We are what we repeatedly do...
Excellence, then is
NOT an act, but a HABIT!

	MON	TUES	WED	THURS	FRI	SAT	SUN
10 *BEFORE* 10 GRATITUDE							
DECLARATIONS							
AUDIO							
READ							
FITNESS							
CONTACT 5 *BY* 5							

THOUGHTS / IDEAS / VISIONS / DREAMS

THIS WEEK'S GOAL / FOCUS

WHAT DO I NEED TO...

STOP _____

_____

START _____

_____

CONTINUE _____

_____

_____

QUOTE OF THE WEEK

"Don't worry about failures, worry about the chances you miss when you don't even try."
JACK CANFIELD

DECLARATION OF THE WEEK

I am solution oriented, and everything is solvable.

WRITE YOUR OWN DECLARATIONS FOR THIS WEEK BELOW:

MAKE IT HAPPEN **MONDAY** ☐	*TAKE ACTION* **TUESDAY** ☐	*WHATEVER IT TAKES* **WEDNESDAY** ☐
TODAY'S GOAL	TODAY'S GOAL	TODAY'S GOAL
5:00	5:00	5:00
5:30	5:30	5:30
6:00	6:00	6:00
6:30	6:30	6:30
7:00	7:00	7:00
7:30	7:30	7:30
8:00	8:00	8:00
8:30	8:30	8:30
9:00	9:00	9:00
9:30	9:30	9:30
10:00	10:00	10:00
10:30	10:30	10:30
11:00	11:00	11:00
11:30	11:30	11:30
12:00	12:00	12:00
12:30	12:30	12:30
1:00	1:00	1:00
1:30	1:30	1:30
2:00	2:00	2:00
2:30	2:30	2:30
3:00	3:00	3:00
3:30	3:30	3:30
4:00	4:00	4:00
4:30	4:30	4:30
5:00	5:00	5:00
5:30	5:30	5:30
6:00	6:00	6:00
6:30	6:30	6:30
7:00	7:00	7:00
7:30	7:30	7:30
8:00	8:00	8:00
8:30	8:30	8:30
9:00	9:00	9:00
9:30	9:30	9:30
10:00	10:00	10:00
10:30	10:30	10:30
11:00	11:00	11:00
11:30	11:30	11:30
12:00	12:00	12:00
12:30	12:30	12:30
PERSONAL TO-DO LIST	**WORK** TO-DO LIST	**FOLLOW UP** LIST
☐	☐	/
☐	☐	/
☐	☐	/
☐	☐	/
☐	☐	/
☐	☐	/
☐	☐	/
☐	☐	/
☐	☐	/

MAXIMIZE YOUR LIFE
P L A N N E R

TODAY'S GOAL	TODAY'S GOAL	TODAY'S GOAL	TODAY'S GOAL

THURSDAY	FRIDAY	SATURDAY	SUNDAY
5:00	5:00	5:00	5:00
5:30	5:30	5:30	5:30
6:00	6:00	6:00	6:00
6:30	6:30	6:30	6:30
7:00	7:00	7:00	7:00
7:30	7:30	7:30	7:30
8:00	8:00	8:00	8:00
8:30	8:30	8:30	8:30
9:00	9:00	9:00	9:00
9:30	9:30	9:30	9:30
10:00	10:00	10:00	10:00
10:30	10:30	10:30	10:30
11:00	11:00	11:00	11:00
11:30	11:30	11:30	11:30
12:00	12:00	12:00	12:00
12:30	12:30	12:30	12:30
1:00	1:00	1:00	1:00
1:30	1:30	1:30	1:30
2:00	2:00	2:00	2:00
2:30	2:30	2:30	2:30
3:00	3:00	3:00	3:00
3:30	3:30	3:30	3:30
4:00	4:00	4:00	4:00
4:30	4:30	4:30	4:30
5:00	5:00	5:00	5:00
5:30	5:30	5:30	5:30
6:00	6:00	6:00	6:00
6:30	6:30	6:30	6:30
7:00	7:00	7:00	7:00
7:30	7:30	7:30	7:30
8:00	8:00	8:00	8:00
8:30	8:30	8:30	8:30
9:00	9:00	9:00	9:00
9:30	9:30	9:30	9:30
10:00	10:00	10:00	10:00
10:30	10:30	10:30	10:30
11:00	11:00	11:00	11:00
11:30	11:30	11:30	11:30
12:00	12:00	12:00	12:00
12:30	12:30	12:30	12:30

We are what we repeatedly do... Excellence, then is NOT an act, but a HABIT!

	MON	TUES	WED	THURS	FRI	SAT	SUN
10 *BEFORE* 10 GRATITUDE							
DECLARATIONS							
AUDIO							
READ							
FITNESS							
CONTACT 5 BY 5							

THOUGHTS / IDEAS / VISIONS / DREAMS

WEEK OF / / - / /

THIS WEEK'S GOAL / FOCUS

WHAT DO I NEED TO...

STOP _____

_____

START _____

_____

CONTINUE _____

_____

QUOTE OF THE WEEK

"Tell me and I forget.
Teach me and I remember.
Involve me and I learn."
BENJAMIN FRANKLIN

DECLARATION OF THE WEEK

I am an irresistible magnet
for all that belongs to
me by divine right.

WRITE YOUR OWN
DECLARATIONS FOR
THIS WEEK BELOW:

MAXIMIZE
YOUR LIFE
P L A N N E R

MAKE IT HAPPEN **MONDAY** ☐	*TAKE ACTION* **TUESDAY** ☐	*WHATEVER IT TAKES* **WEDNESDAY** ☐
TODAY'S GOAL	TODAY'S GOAL	TODAY'S GOAL
5:00	5:00	5:00
5:30	5:30	5:30
6:00	6:00	6:00
6:30	6:30	6:30
7:00	7:00	7:00
7:30	7:30	7:30
8:00	8:00	8:00
8:30	8:30	8:30
9:00	9:00	9:00
9:30	9:30	9:30
10:00	10:00	10:00
10:30	10:30	10:30
11:00	11:00	11:00
11:30	11:30	11:30
12:00	12:00	12:00
12:30	12:30	12:30
1:00	1:00	1:00
1:30	1:30	1:30
2:00	2:00	2:00
2:30	2:30	2:30
3:00	3:00	3:00
3:30	3:30	3:30
4:00	4:00	4:00
4:30	4:30	4:30
5:00	5:00	5:00
5:30	5:30	5:30
6:00	6:00	6:00
6:30	6:30	6:30
7:00	7:00	7:00
7:30	7:30	7:30
8:00	8:00	8:00
8:30	8:30	8:30
9:00	9:00	9:00
9:30	9:30	9:30
10:00	10:00	10:00
10:30	10:30	10:30
11:00	11:00	11:00
11:30	11:30	11:30
12:00	12:00	12:00
12:30	12:30	12:30
PERSONAL TO-DO LIST	**WORK** TO-DO LIST	**FOLLOW UP** LIST
☐	☐	/
☐	☐	/
☐	☐	/
☐	☐	/
☐	☐	/
☐	☐	/
☐	☐	/
☐	☐	/
☐	☐	/
☐	☐	/

TURN IT UP
THURSDAY ☐

FINISH STRONG
FRIDAY ☐

STEP IT UP
SATURDAY ☐

SOULFUL
SUNDAY ☐

THURSDAY — TODAY'S GOAL

FRIDAY — TODAY'S GOAL

SATURDAY — TODAY'S GOAL

SUNDAY — TODAY'S GOAL

THURSDAY	FRIDAY	SATURDAY	SUNDAY
5:00	5:00	5:00	5:00
5:30	5:30	5:30	5:30
6:00	6:00	6:00	6:00
6:30	6:30	6:30	6:30
7:00	7:00	7:00	7:00
7:30	7:30	7:30	7:30
8:00	8:00	8:00	8:00
8:30	8:30	8:30	8:30
9:00	9:00	9:00	9:00
9:30	9:30	9:30	9:30
10:00	10:00	10:00	10:00
10:30	10:30	10:30	10:30
11:00	11:00	11:00	11:00
11:30	11:30	11:30	11:30
12:00	12:00	12:00	12:00
12:30	12:30	12:30	12:30
1:00	1:00	1:00	1:00
1:30	1:30	1:30	1:30
2:00	2:00	2:00	2:00
2:30	2:30	2:30	2:30
3:00	3:00	3:00	3:00
3:30	3:30	3:30	3:30
4:00	4:00	4:00	4:00
4:30	4:30	4:30	4:30
5:00	5:00	5:00	5:00
5:30	5:30	5:30	5:30
6:00	6:00	6:00	6:00
6:30	6:30	6:30	6:30
7:00	7:00	7:00	7:00
7:30	7:30	7:30	7:30
8:00	8:00	8:00	8:00
8:30	8:30	8:30	8:30
9:00	9:00	9:00	9:00
9:30	9:30	9:30	9:30
10:00	10:00	10:00	10:00
10:30	10:30	10:30	10:30
11:00	11:00	11:00	11:00
11:30	11:30	11:30	11:30
12:00	12:00	12:00	12:00
12:30	12:30	12:30	12:30

We are what we repeatedly do... Excellence, then is NOT an act, but a HABIT!

	MON	TUES	WED	THURS	FRI	SAT	SUN
10 *BEFORE* 10 GRATITUDE							
DECLARATIONS							
AUDIO							
READ							
FITNESS							
CONTACT 5 *BY* 5							

THOUGHTS / IDEAS / VISIONS / DREAMS

THIS WEEK'S GOAL / FOCUS

WHAT DO I NEED TO...

STOP _____

_____

START _____

_____

CONTINUE _____

_____

_____

QUOTE OF THE WEEK

"It is during our darkest moments that we must focus to see the light."
ARISTOTLE

DECLARATION OF THE WEEK

I am a light that gives hope, inspiration, and belief for others to achieve their dreams.

WRITE YOUR OWN DECLARATIONS FOR THIS WEEK BELOW:

_____
_____
_____
_____
_____
_____
_____
_____
_____
_____
_____
_____
_____
_____
_____
_____
_____
_____

MAXIMIZE YOUR LIFE PLANNER

MAKE IT HAPPEN
MONDAY ☐
TODAY'S GOAL

Time	
5:00	
5:30	
6:00	
6:30	
7:00	
7:30	
8:00	
8:30	
9:00	
9:30	
10:00	
10:30	
11:00	
11:30	
12:00	
12:30	
1:00	
1:30	
2:00	
2:30	
3:00	
3:30	
4:00	
4:30	
5:00	
5:30	
6:00	
6:30	
7:00	
7:30	
8:00	
8:30	
9:00	
9:30	
10:00	
10:30	
11:00	
11:30	
12:00	
12:30	

PERSONAL TO-DO LIST
☐
☐
☐
☐
☐
☐
☐
☐
☐

TAKE ACTION
TUESDAY ☐
TODAY'S GOAL

Time	
5:00	
5:30	
6:00	
6:30	
7:00	
7:30	
8:00	
8:30	
9:00	
9:30	
10:00	
10:30	
11:00	
11:30	
12:00	
12:30	
1:00	
1:30	
2:00	
2:30	
3:00	
3:30	
4:00	
4:30	
5:00	
5:30	
6:00	
6:30	
7:00	
7:30	
8:00	
8:30	
9:00	
9:30	
10:00	
10:30	
11:00	
11:30	
12:00	
12:30	

WORK TO-DO LIST
☐
☐
☐
☐
☐
☐
☐
☐

WHATEVER IT TAKES
WEDNESDAY ☐
TODAY'S GOAL

Time	
5:00	
5:30	
6:00	
6:30	
7:00	
7:30	
8:00	
8:30	
9:00	
9:30	
10:00	
10:30	
11:00	
11:30	
12:00	
12:30	
1:00	
1:30	
2:00	
2:30	
3:00	
3:30	
4:00	
4:30	
5:00	
5:30	
6:00	
6:30	
7:00	
7:30	
8:00	
8:30	
9:00	
9:30	
10:00	
10:30	
11:00	
11:30	
12:00	
12:30	

FOLLOW UP LIST
/
/
/
/
/
/
/
/
/

THURSDAY — TODAY'S GOAL

FRIDAY — TODAY'S GOAL

SATURDAY — TODAY'S GOAL

SUNDAY — TODAY'S GOAL

Each day column contains time slots:

5:00, 5:30, 6:00, 6:30, 7:00, 7:30, 8:00, 8:30, 9:00, 9:30, 10:00, 10:30, 11:00, 11:30, 12:00, 12:30, 1:00, 1:30, 2:00, 2:30, 3:00, 3:30, 4:00, 4:30, 5:00, 5:30, 6:00, 6:30, 7:00, 7:30, 8:00, 8:30, 9:00, 9:30, 10:00, 10:30, 11:00, 11:30, 12:00, 12:30

We are what we repeatedly do... Excellence, then is NOT an act, but a HABIT!	MON	TUES	WED	THURS	FRI	SAT	SUN
10 *BEFORE* 10 GRATITUDE							
DECLARATIONS							
AUDIO							
READ							
FITNESS							
CONTACT 5 *BY* 5							

THOUGHTS / IDEAS / VISIONS / DREAMS

WEEK OF
/ / - / /

THIS WEEK'S GOAL / FOCUS

WHAT DO I NEED TO...

STOP _____
_____
START _____
_____
CONTINUE _____
_____

QUOTE OF THE WEEK
"Do not go where the path may lead, go instead where there is no path and leave a trail."
RALPH WALDO EMERSON

DECLARATION OF THE WEEK
I encounter happiness in all my relationships, and I love these encounters.

WRITE YOUR OWN DECLARATIONS FOR THIS WEEK BELOW:
_____
_____
_____
_____
_____
_____
_____
_____
_____
_____
_____
_____
_____
_____
_____

MAXIMIZE YOUR LIFE PLANNER

MAKE IT HAPPEN MONDAY	TAKE ACTION TUESDAY	WHATEVER IT TAKES WEDNESDAY
TODAY'S GOAL	TODAY'S GOAL	TODAY'S GOAL
5:00	5:00	5:00
5:30	5:30	5:30
6:00	6:00	6:00
6:30	6:30	6:30
7:00	7:00	7:00
7:30	7:30	7:30
8:00	8:00	8:00
8:30	8:30	8:30
9:00	9:00	9:00
9:30	9:30	9:30
10:00	10:00	10:00
10:30	10:30	10:30
11:00	11:00	11:00
11:30	11:30	11:30
12:00	12:00	12:00
12:30	12:30	12:30
1:00	1:00	1:00
1:30	1:30	1:30
2:00	2:00	2:00
2:30	2:30	2:30
3:00	3:00	3:00
3:30	3:30	3:30
4:00	4:00	4:00
4:30	4:30	4:30
5:00	5:00	5:00
5:30	5:30	5:30
6:00	6:00	6:00
6:30	6:30	6:30
7:00	7:00	7:00
7:30	7:30	7:30
8:00	8:00	8:00
8:30	8:30	8:30
9:00	9:00	9:00
9:30	9:30	9:30
10:00	10:00	10:00
10:30	10:30	10:30
11:00	11:00	11:00
11:30	11:30	11:30
12:00	12:00	12:00
12:30	12:30	12:30

PERSONAL TO-DO LIST	WORK TO-DO LIST	FOLLOW UP LIST
☐	☐	/
☐	☐	/
☐	☐	/
☐	☐	/
☐	☐	/
☐	☐	/
☐	☐	/
☐	☐	/
☐	☐	/

TURN IT UP **THURSDAY** ☐	FINISH STRONG **FRIDAY** ☐	STEP IT UP **SATURDAY** ☐	SOULFUL **SUNDAY** ☐
TODAY'S GOAL	TODAY'S GOAL	TODAY'S GOAL	TODAY'S GOAL

Thursday	Friday	Saturday	Sunday
5:00	5:00	5:00	5:00
5:30	5:30	5:30	5:30
6:00	6:00	6:00	6:00
6:30	6:30	6:30	6:30
7:00	7:00	7:00	7:00
7:30	7:30	7:30	7:30
8:00	8:00	8:00	8:00
8:30	8:30	8:30	8:30
9:00	9:00	9:00	9:00
9:30	9:30	9:30	9:30
10:00	10:00	10:00	10:00
10:30	10:30	10:30	10:30
11:00	11:00	11:00	11:00
11:30	11:30	11:30	11:30
12:00	12:00	12:00	12:00
12:30	12:30	12:30	12:30
1:00	1:00	1:00	1:00
1:30	1:30	1:30	1:30
2:00	2:00	2:00	2:00
2:30	2:30	2:30	2:30
3:00	3:00	3:00	3:00
3:30	3:30	3:30	3:30
4:00	4:00	4:00	4:00
4:30	4:30	4:30	4:30
5:00	5:00	5:00	5:00
5:30	5:30	5:30	5:30
6:00	6:00	6:00	6:00
6:30	6:30	6:30	6:30
7:00	7:00	7:00	7:00
7:30	7:30	7:30	7:30
8:00	8:00	8:00	8:00
8:30	8:30	8:30	8:30
9:00	9:00	9:00	9:00
9:30	9:30	9:30	9:30
10:00	10:00	10:00	10:00
10:30	10:30	10:30	10:30
11:00	11:00	11:00	11:00
11:30	11:30	11:30	11:30
12:00	12:00	12:00	12:00
12:30	12:30	12:30	12:30

We are what we repeatedly do... Excellence, then is NOT an act, but a HABIT!	MON	TUES	WED	THURS	FRI	SAT	SUN
10 BEFORE **10** GRATITUDE							
DECLARATIONS							
AUDIO							
READ							
FITNESS							
CONTACT 5 BY **5**							

THOUGHTS / IDEAS / VISIONS / DREAMS

THIS WEEK'S GOAL / FOCUS

WHAT DO I NEED TO...

STOP _____

_____

START _____

_____

CONTINUE _____

_____

QUOTE OF THE WEEK

*"You have brains in your head.
You have feet in your shoes.
You can steer yourself any
direction you choose."*
DR. SEUSS

DECLARATION OF THE WEEK

*I am surrounded by go-getters
and innovators who inspire
me and help me grow.*

**WRITE YOUR OWN
DECLARATIONS FOR
THIS WEEK BELOW:**

_____

_____

_____

_____

_____

_____

_____

_____

_____

_____

_____

_____

_____

_____

_____

MAXIMIZE
YOUR LIFE
PLANNER

MAKE IT HAPPEN **MONDAY** ☐	*TAKE ACTION* **TUESDAY** ☐	*WHATEVER IT TAKES* **WEDNESDAY** ☐
TODAY'S GOAL	TODAY'S GOAL	TODAY'S GOAL
5:00	5:00	5:00
5:30	5:30	5:30
6:00	6:00	6:00
6:30	6:30	6:30
7:00	7:00	7:00
7:30	7:30	7:30
8:00	8:00	8:00
8:30	8:30	8:30
9:00	9:00	9:00
9:30	9:30	9:30
10:00	10:00	10:00
10:30	10:30	10:30
11:00	11:00	11:00
11:30	11:30	11:30
12:00	12:00	12:00
12:30	12:30	12:30
1:00	1:00	1:00
1:30	1:30	1:30
2:00	2:00	2:00
2:30	2:30	2:30
3:00	3:00	3:00
3:30	3:30	3:30
4:00	4:00	4:00
4:30	4:30	4:30
5:00	5:00	5:00
5:30	5:30	5:30
6:00	6:00	6:00
6:30	6:30	6:30
7:00	7:00	7:00
7:30	7:30	7:30
8:00	8:00	8:00
8:30	8:30	8:30
9:00	9:00	9:00
9:30	9:30	9:30
10:00	10:00	10:00
10:30	10:30	10:30
11:00	11:00	11:00
11:30	11:30	11:30
12:00	12:00	12:00
12:30	12:30	12:30
PERSONAL TO-DO LIST	**WORK** TO-DO LIST	**FOLLOW UP** LIST
☐	☐	/
☐	☐	/
☐	☐	/
☐	☐	/
☐	☐	/
☐	☐	/
☐	☐	/
☐	☐	/
☐	☐	/

TURN IT UP **THURSDAY** ☐	FINISH STRONG **FRIDAY** ☐	STEP IT UP **SATURDAY** ☐	SOULFUL **SUNDAY** ☐
TODAY'S GOAL	TODAY'S GOAL	TODAY'S GOAL	TODAY'S GOAL

THURSDAY	FRIDAY	SATURDAY	SUNDAY
5:00	5:00	5:00	5:00
5:30	5:30	5:30	5:30
6:00	6:00	6:00	6:00
6:30	6:30	6:30	6:30
7:00	7:00	7:00	7:00
7:30	7:30	7:30	7:30
8:00	8:00	8:00	8:00
8:30	8:30	8:30	8:30
9:00	9:00	9:00	9:00
9:30	9:30	9:30	9:30
10:00	10:00	10:00	10:00
10:30	10:30	10:30	10:30
11:00	11:00	11:00	11:00
11:30	11:30	11:30	11:30
12:00	12:00	12:00	12:00
12:30	12:30	12:30	12:30
1:00	1:00	1:00	1:00
1:30	1:30	1:30	1:30
2:00	2:00	2:00	2:00
2:30	2:30	2:30	2:30
3:00	3:00	3:00	3:00
3:30	3:30	3:30	3:30
4:00	4:00	4:00	4:00
4:30	4:30	4:30	4:30
5:00	5:00	5:00	5:00
5:30	5:30	5:30	5:30
6:00	6:00	6:00	6:00
6:30	6:30	6:30	6:30
7:00	7:00	7:00	7:00
7:30	7:30	7:30	7:30
8:00	8:00	8:00	8:00
8:30	8:30	8:30	8:30
9:00	9:00	9:00	9:00
9:30	9:30	9:30	9:30
10:00	10:00	10:00	10:00
10:30	10:30	10:30	10:30
11:00	11:00	11:00	11:00
11:30	11:30	11:30	11:30
12:00	12:00	12:00	12:00
12:30	12:30	12:30	12:30

We are what we repeatedly do... Excellence, then is NOT an act, but a HABIT!	MON	TUES	WED	THURS	FRI	SAT	SUN
10 *BEFORE* **10 GRATITUDE**							
DECLARATIONS							
AUDIO							
READ							
FITNESS							
CONTACT 5 *BY* **5**							

THOUGHTS / IDEAS / VISIONS / DREAMS

WEEK OF
/ / - / /

THIS WEEK'S GOAL / FOCUS

WHAT DO I NEED TO...

STOP _____
_____

START _____
_____

CONTINUE _____
_____

QUOTE OF THE WEEK
"The greatest glory in living lies not in never falling, but in rising every time we fall."
NELSON MANDELA

DECLARATION OF THE WEEK
I am grateful for my healthy body. Peace flows through my body, mind, and soul.

WRITE YOUR OWN DECLARATIONS FOR THIS WEEK BELOW:

_____
_____
_____
_____
_____
_____
_____
_____
_____
_____
_____
_____
_____
_____
_____
_____
_____

MAXIMIZE YOUR LIFE PLANNER

MAKE IT HAPPEN **MONDAY** ☐	*TAKE ACTION* **TUESDAY** ☐	*WHATEVER IT TAKES* **WEDNESDAY** ☐
TODAY'S GOAL	TODAY'S GOAL	TODAY'S GOAL
5:00	5:00	5:00
5:30	5:30	5:30
6:00	6:00	6:00
6:30	6:30	6:30
7:00	7:00	7:00
7:30	7:30	7:30
8:00	8:00	8:00
8:30	8:30	8:30
9:00	9:00	9:00
9:30	9:30	9:30
10:00	10:00	10:00
10:30	10:30	10:30
11:00	11:00	11:00
11:30	11:30	11:30
12:00	12:00	12:00
12:30	12:30	12:30
1:00	1:00	1:00
1:30	1:30	1:30
2:00	2:00	2:00
2:30	2:30	2:30
3:00	3:00	3:00
3:30	3:30	3:30
4:00	4:00	4:00
4:30	4:30	4:30
5:00	5:00	5:00
5:30	5:30	5:30
6:00	6:00	6:00
6:30	6:30	6:30
7:00	7:00	7:00
7:30	7:30	7:30
8:00	8:00	8:00
8:30	8:30	8:30
9:00	9:00	9:00
9:30	9:30	9:30
10:00	10:00	10:00
10:30	10:30	10:30
11:00	11:00	11:00
11:30	11:30	11:30
12:00	12:00	12:00
12:30	12:30	12:30
PERSONAL TO-DO LIST	**WORK** TO-DO LIST	**FOLLOW UP** LIST
☐	☐	/
☐	☐	/
☐	☐	/
☐	☐	/
☐	☐	/
☐	☐	/
☐	☐	/
☐	☐	/
☐	☐	/

TURN IT UP **THURSDAY** ☐	FINISH STRONG **FRIDAY** ☐	STEP IT UP **SATURDAY** ☐	SOULFUL **SUNDAY** ☐
TODAY'S GOAL	TODAY'S GOAL	TODAY'S GOAL	TODAY'S GOAL

THURSDAY	FRIDAY	SATURDAY	SUNDAY
5:00	5:00	5:00	5:00
5:30	5:30	5:30	5:30
6:00	6:00	6:00	6:00
6:30	6:30	6:30	6:30
7:00	7:00	7:00	7:00
7:30	7:30	7:30	7:30
8:00	8:00	8:00	8:00
8:30	8:30	8:30	8:30
9:00	9:00	9:00	9:00
9:30	9:30	9:30	9:30
10:00	10:00	10:00	10:00
10:30	10:30	10:30	10:30
11:00	11:00	11:00	11:00
11:30	11:30	11:30	11:30
12:00	12:00	12:00	12:00
12:30	12:30	12:30	12:30
1:00	1:00	1:00	1:00
1:30	1:30	1:30	1:30
2:00	2:00	2:00	2:00
2:30	2:30	2:30	2:30
3:00	3:00	3:00	3:00
3:30	3:30	3:30	3:30
4:00	4:00	4:00	4:00
4:30	4:30	4:30	4:30
5:00	5:00	5:00	5:00
5:30	5:30	5:30	5:30
6:00	6:00	6:00	6:00
6:30	6:30	6:30	6:30
7:00	7:00	7:00	7:00
7:30	7:30	7:30	7:30
8:00	8:00	8:00	8:00
8:30	8:30	8:30	8:30
9:00	9:00	9:00	9:00
9:30	9:30	9:30	9:30
10:00	10:00	10:00	10:00
10:30	10:30	10:30	10:30
11:00	11:00	11:00	11:00
11:30	11:30	11:30	11:30
12:00	12:00	12:00	12:00
12:30	12:30	12:30	12:30

We are what we repeatedly do... Excellence, then is NOT an act, but a HABIT!	MON	TUES	WED	THURS	FRI	SAT	SUN
10 *BEFORE* 10 GRATITUDE							
DECLARATIONS							
AUDIO							
READ							
FITNESS							
CONTACT 5 *BY* 5							

THOUGHTS / IDEAS / VISIONS / DREAMS

WEEK OF

/ / - / /

THIS WEEK'S GOAL / FOCUS

WHAT DO I NEED TO...

STOP _____

_____

START _____

_____

CONTINUE _____

_____

_____

QUOTE OF THE WEEK

"In the end, it's not the years in your life that count. It's the life in your years."
ABRAHAM LINCOLN

DECLARATION OF THE WEEK

God's grace and love is working through me.

WRITE YOUR OWN DECLARATIONS FOR THIS WEEK BELOW:

_____
_____
_____
_____
_____
_____
_____
_____
_____
_____
_____
_____
_____
_____
_____
_____
_____
_____
_____

MAXIMIZE YOUR LIFE PLANNER

MAKE IT HAPPEN **MONDAY**	TAKE ACTION **TUESDAY**	WHATEVER IT TAKES **WEDNESDAY**
TODAY'S GOAL	TODAY'S GOAL	TODAY'S GOAL

Time	Monday	Tuesday	Wednesday
5:00			
5:30			
6:00			
6:30			
7:00			
7:30			
8:00			
8:30			
9:00			
9:30			
10:00			
10:30			
11:00			
11:30			
12:00			
12:30			
1:00			
1:30			
2:00			
2:30			
3:00			
3:30			
4:00			
4:30			
5:00			
5:30			
6:00			
6:30			
7:00			
7:30			
8:00			
8:30			
9:00			
9:30			
10:00			
10:30			
11:00			
11:30			
12:00			
12:30			

PERSONAL TO-DO LIST	**WORK** TO-DO LIST	**FOLLOW UP** LIST
☐	☐	/
☐	☐	/
☐	☐	/
☐	☐	/
☐	☐	/
☐	☐	/
☐	☐	/
☐	☐	/
☐	☐	/

THURSDAY

TODAY'S GOAL

5:00	
5:30	
6:00	
6:30	
7:00	
7:30	
8:00	
8:30	
9:00	
9:30	
10:00	
10:30	
11:00	
11:30	
12:00	
12:30	
1:00	
1:30	
2:00	
2:30	
3:00	
3:30	
4:00	
4:30	
5:00	
5:30	
6:00	
6:30	
7:00	
7:30	
8:00	
8:30	
9:00	
9:30	
10:00	
10:30	
11:00	
11:30	
12:00	
12:30	

FRIDAY

TODAY'S GOAL

5:00	
5:30	
6:00	
6:30	
7:00	
7:30	
8:00	
8:30	
9:00	
9:30	
10:00	
10:30	
11:00	
11:30	
12:00	
12:30	
1:00	
1:30	
2:00	
2:30	
3:00	
3:30	
4:00	
4:30	
5:00	
5:30	
6:00	
6:30	
7:00	
7:30	
8:00	
8:30	
9:00	
9:30	
10:00	
10:30	
11:00	
11:30	
12:00	
12:30	

SATURDAY

TODAY'S GOAL

5:00	
5:30	
6:00	
6:30	
7:00	
7:30	
8:00	
8:30	
9:00	
9:30	
10:00	
10:30	
11:00	
11:30	
12:00	
12:30	
1:00	
1:30	
2:00	
2:30	
3:00	
3:30	
4:00	
4:30	
5:00	
5:30	
6:00	
6:30	
7:00	
7:30	
8:00	
8:30	
9:00	
9:30	
10:00	
10:30	
11:00	
11:30	
12:00	
12:30	

SUNDAY

TODAY'S GOAL

5:00	
5:30	
6:00	
6:30	
7:00	
7:30	
8:00	
8:30	
9:00	
9:30	
10:00	
10:30	
11:00	
11:30	
12:00	
12:30	
1:00	
1:30	
2:00	
2:30	
3:00	
3:30	
4:00	
4:30	
5:00	
5:30	
6:00	
6:30	
7:00	
7:30	
8:00	
8:30	
9:00	
9:30	
10:00	
10:30	
11:00	
11:30	
12:00	
12:30	

We are what we repeatedly do... Excellence, then is NOT an act, but a HABIT!

	MON	TUES	WED	THURS	FRI	SAT	SUN
10 *BEFORE* 10 GRATITUDE							
DECLARATIONS							
AUDIO							
READ							
FITNESS							
CONTACT 5 *BY* 5							

THOUGHTS / IDEAS / VISIONS / DREAMS

THIS WEEK'S GOAL / FOCUS

WHAT DO I NEED TO...

STOP _____

_____

START _____

_____

CONTINUE _____

_____

QUOTE OF THE WEEK

"Never let the fear of striking out keep you from playing the game."
BABE RUTH

DECLARATION OF THE WEEK

I love being physically fit and having the power to create change.

WRITE YOUR OWN DECLARATIONS FOR THIS WEEK BELOW:

_____
_____
_____
_____
_____
_____
_____
_____
_____
_____
_____
_____
_____
_____
_____
_____
_____
_____
_____

MAXIMIZE
YOUR LIFE
P L A N N E R

MAKE IT HAPPEN MONDAY ☐	TAKE ACTION TUESDAY ☐	WHATEVER IT TAKES WEDNESDAY ☐
TODAY'S GOAL	TODAY'S GOAL	TODAY'S GOAL
5:00	5:00	5:00
5:30	5:30	5:30
6:00	6:00	6:00
6:30	6:30	6:30
7:00	7:00	7:00
7:30	7:30	7:30
8:00	8:00	8:00
8:30	8:30	8:30
9:00	9:00	9:00
9:30	9:30	9:30
10:00	10:00	10:00
10:30	10:30	10:30
11:00	11:00	11:00
11:30	11:30	11:30
12:00	12:00	12:00
12:30	12:30	12:30
1:00	1:00	1:00
1:30	1:30	1:30
2:00	2:00	2:00
2:30	2:30	2:30
3:00	3:00	3:00
3:30	3:30	3:30
4:00	4:00	4:00
4:30	4:30	4:30
5:00	5:00	5:00
5:30	5:30	5:30
6:00	6:00	6:00
6:30	6:30	6:30
7:00	7:00	7:00
7:30	7:30	7:30
8:00	8:00	8:00
8:30	8:30	8:30
9:00	9:00	9:00
9:30	9:30	9:30
10:00	10:00	10:00
10:30	10:30	10:30
11:00	11:00	11:00
11:30	11:30	11:30
12:00	12:00	12:00
12:30	12:30	12:30
PERSONAL TO-DO LIST	**WORK** TO-DO LIST	**FOLLOW UP** LIST
☐	☐	/
☐	☐	/
☐	☐	/
☐	☐	/
☐	☐	/
☐	☐	/
☐	☐	/
☐	☐	/
☐	☐	/

TURN IT UP THURSDAY		FINISH STRONG FRIDAY		STEP IT UP SATURDAY		SOULFUL SUNDAY	
TODAY'S GOAL		TODAY'S GOAL		TODAY'S GOAL		TODAY'S GOAL	
5:00		5:00		5:00		5:00	
5:30		5:30		5:30		5:30	
6:00		6:00		6:00		6:00	
6:30		6:30		6:30		6:30	
7:00		7:00		7:00		7:00	
7:30		7:30		7:30		7:30	
8:00		8:00		8:00		8:00	
8:30		8:30		8:30		8:30	
9:00		9:00		9:00		9:00	
9:30		9:30		9:30		9:30	
10:00		10:00		10:00		10:00	
10:30		10:30		10:30		10:30	
11:00		11:00		11:00		11:00	
11:30		11:30		11:30		11:30	
12:00		12:00		12:00		12:00	
12:30		12:30		12:30		12:30	
1:00		1:00		1:00		1:00	
1:30		1:30		1:30		1:30	
2:00		2:00		2:00		2:00	
2:30		2:30		2:30		2:30	
3:00		3:00		3:00		3:00	
3:30		3:30		3:30		3:30	
4:00		4:00		4:00		4:00	
4:30		4:30		4:30		4:30	
5:00		5:00		5:00		5:00	
5:30		5:30		5:30		5:30	
6:00		6:00		6:00		6:00	
6:30		6:30		6:30		6:30	
7:00		7:00		7:00		7:00	
7:30		7:30		7:30		7:30	
8:00		8:00		8:00		8:00	
8:30		8:30		8:30		8:30	
9:00		9:00		9:00		9:00	
9:30		9:30		9:30		9:30	
10:00		10:00		10:00		10:00	
10:30		10:30		10:30		10:30	
11:00		11:00		11:00		11:00	
11:30		11:30		11:30		11:30	
12:00		12:00		12:00		12:00	
12:30		12:30		12:30		12:30	

We are what we repeatedly do... Excellence, then is NOT an act, but a HABIT!	MON	TUES	WED	THURS	FRI	SAT	SUN
10 BEFORE 10 GRATITUDE							
DECLARATIONS							
AUDIO							
READ							
FITNESS							
CONTACT 5 BY 5							

THOUGHTS / IDEAS / VISIONS / DREAMS

WEEK OF
/ / - / /

THIS WEEK'S GOAL / FOCUS

WHAT DO I NEED TO...

STOP _____

_____

START _____

_____

CONTINUE _____

_____

QUOTE OF THE WEEK

"Many of life's failures are people who did not realize how close they were to success when they gave up."
THOMAS A. EDISON

DECLARATION OF THE WEEK

Wealth flows into my life very smoothly.

WRITE YOUR OWN DECLARATIONS FOR THIS WEEK BELOW:

_____
_____
_____
_____
_____
_____
_____
_____
_____
_____
_____
_____
_____
_____

MAKE IT HAPPEN
MONDAY ☐

TODAY'S GOAL

TAKE ACTION
TUESDAY ☐

TODAY'S GOAL

WHATEVER IT TAKES
WEDNESDAY ☐

TODAY'S GOAL

MONDAY	TUESDAY	WEDNESDAY
5:00	5:00	5:00
5:30	5:30	5:30
6:00	6:00	6:00
6:30	6:30	6:30
7:00	7:00	7:00
7:30	7:30	7:30
8:00	8:00	8:00
8:30	8:30	8:30
9:00	9:00	9:00
9:30	9:30	9:30
10:00	10:00	10:00
10:30	10:30	10:30
11:00	11:00	11:00
11:30	11:30	11:30
12:00	12:00	12:00
12:30	12:30	12:30
1:00	1:00	1:00
1:30	1:30	1:30
2:00	2:00	2:00
2:30	2:30	2:30
3:00	3:00	3:00
3:30	3:30	3:30
4:00	4:00	4:00
4:30	4:30	4:30
5:00	5:00	5:00
5:30	5:30	5:30
6:00	6:00	6:00
6:30	6:30	6:30
7:00	7:00	7:00
7:30	7:30	7:30
8:00	8:00	8:00
8:30	8:30	8:30
9:00	9:00	9:00
9:30	9:30	9:30
10:00	10:00	10:00
10:30	10:30	10:30
11:00	11:00	11:00
11:30	11:30	11:30
12:00	12:00	12:00
12:30	12:30	12:30

PERSONAL TO-DO LIST	WORK TO-DO LIST	FOLLOW UP LIST
☐	☐	/
☐	☐	/
☐	☐	/
☐	☐	/
☐	☐	/
☐	☐	/
☐	☐	/
☐	☐	/
☐	☐	/

MAXIMIZE YOUR LIFE
P L A N N E R

TURN IT UP THURSDAY ☐	FINISH STRONG FRIDAY ☐	STEP IT UP SATURDAY ☐	SOULFUL SUNDAY ☐
TODAY'S GOAL	TODAY'S GOAL	TODAY'S GOAL	TODAY'S GOAL

THURSDAY	FRIDAY	SATURDAY	SUNDAY
5:00	5:00	5:00	5:00
5:30	5:30	5:30	5:30
6:00	6:00	6:00	6:00
6:30	6:30	6:30	6:30
7:00	7:00	7:00	7:00
7:30	7:30	7:30	7:30
8:00	8:00	8:00	8:00
8:30	8:30	8:30	8:30
9:00	9:00	9:00	9:00
9:30	9:30	9:30	9:30
10:00	10:00	10:00	10:00
10:30	10:30	10:30	10:30
11:00	11:00	11:00	11:00
11:30	11:30	11:30	11:30
12:00	12:00	12:00	12:00
12:30	12:30	12:30	12:30
1:00	1:00	1:00	1:00
1:30	1:30	1:30	1:30
2:00	2:00	2:00	2:00
2:30	2:30	2:30	2:30
3:00	3:00	3:00	3:00
3:30	3:30	3:30	3:30
4:00	4:00	4:00	4:00
4:30	4:30	4:30	4:30
5:00	5:00	5:00	5:00
5:30	5:30	5:30	5:30
6:00	6:00	6:00	6:00
6:30	6:30	6:30	6:30
7:00	7:00	7:00	7:00
7:30	7:30	7:30	7:30
8:00	8:00	8:00	8:00
8:30	8:30	8:30	8:30
9:00	9:00	9:00	9:00
9:30	9:30	9:30	9:30
10:00	10:00	10:00	10:00
10:30	10:30	10:30	10:30
11:00	11:00	11:00	11:00
11:30	11:30	11:30	11:30
12:00	12:00	12:00	12:00
12:30	12:30	12:30	12:30

We are what we repeatedly do... Excellence, then is NOT an act, but a HABIT!	MON	TUES	WED	THURS	FRI	SAT	SUN
10 BEFORE 10 GRATITUDE							
DECLARATIONS							
AUDIO							
READ							
FITNESS							
CONTACT 5 BY 5							

THOUGHTS / IDEAS / VISIONS / DREAMS

WEEK OF

/ / - / /

THIS WEEK'S GOAL / FOCUS

WHAT DO I NEED TO...

STOP _____

_____

START _____

_____

CONTINUE _____

_____

QUOTE OF THE WEEK

"Stop trying to find someone to validate what you know God already put inside of you."

MYRON GOLDEN

DECLARATION OF THE WEEK

I love seeing God use me to show others how great he is.

WRITE YOUR OWN DECLARATIONS FOR THIS WEEK BELOW:

_____
_____
_____
_____
_____
_____
_____
_____
_____
_____
_____
_____
_____
_____
_____
_____
_____
_____
_____
_____
_____

MAXIMIZE YOUR LIFE PLANNER

MAKE IT HAPPEN MONDAY	*TAKE ACTION* TUESDAY	*WHATEVER IT TAKES* WEDNESDAY
TODAY'S GOAL	TODAY'S GOAL	TODAY'S GOAL
5:00	5:00	5:00
5:30	5:30	5:30
6:00	6:00	6:00
6:30	6:30	6:30
7:00	7:00	7:00
7:30	7:30	7:30
8:00	8:00	8:00
8:30	8:30	8:30
9:00	9:00	9:00
9:30	9:30	9:30
10:00	10:00	10:00
10:30	10:30	10:30
11:00	11:00	11:00
11:30	11:30	11:30
12:00	12:00	12:00
12:30	12:30	12:30
1:00	1:00	1:00
1:30	1:30	1:30
2:00	2:00	2:00
2:30	2:30	2:30
3:00	3:00	3:00
3:30	3:30	3:30
4:00	4:00	4:00
4:30	4:30	4:30
5:00	5:00	5:00
5:30	5:30	5:30
6:00	6:00	6:00
6:30	6:30	6:30
7:00	7:00	7:00
7:30	7:30	7:30
8:00	8:00	8:00
8:30	8:30	8:30
9:00	9:00	9:00
9:30	9:30	9:30
10:00	10:00	10:00
10:30	10:30	10:30
11:00	11:00	11:00
11:30	11:30	11:30
12:00	12:00	12:00
12:30	12:30	12:30

PERSONAL TO-DO LIST	**WORK** TO-DO LIST	**FOLLOW UP** LIST
☐	☐	/
☐	☐	/
☐	☐	/
☐	☐	/
☐	☐	/
☐	☐	/
☐	☐	/
☐	☐	/
☐	☐	/

TURN IT UP **THURSDAY** ☐	FINISH STRONG **FRIDAY** ☐	STEP IT UP **SATURDAY** ☐	SOULFUL **SUNDAY** ☐
TODAY'S GOAL	TODAY'S GOAL	TODAY'S GOAL	TODAY'S GOAL

THURSDAY	FRIDAY	SATURDAY	SUNDAY
5:00	5:00	5:00	5:00
5:30	5:30	5:30	5:30
6:00	6:00	6:00	6:00
6:30	6:30	6:30	6:30
7:00	7:00	7:00	7:00
7:30	7:30	7:30	7:30
8:00	8:00	8:00	8:00
8:30	8:30	8:30	8:30
9:00	9:00	9:00	9:00
9:30	9:30	9:30	9:30
10:00	10:00	10:00	10:00
10:30	10:30	10:30	10:30
11:00	11:00	11:00	11:00
11:30	11:30	11:30	11:30
12:00	12:00	12:00	12:00
12:30	12:30	12:30	12:30
1:00	1:00	1:00	1:00
1:30	1:30	1:30	1:30
2:00	2:00	2:00	2:00
2:30	2:30	2:30	2:30
3:00	3:00	3:00	3:00
3:30	3:30	3:30	3:30
4:00	4:00	4:00	4:00
4:30	4:30	4:30	4:30
5:00	5:00	5:00	5:00
5:30	5:30	5:30	5:30
6:00	6:00	6:00	6:00
6:30	6:30	6:30	6:30
7:00	7:00	7:00	7:00
7:30	7:30	7:30	7:30
8:00	8:00	8:00	8:00
8:30	8:30	8:30	8:30
9:00	9:00	9:00	9:00
9:30	9:30	9:30	9:30
10:00	10:00	10:00	10:00
10:30	10:30	10:30	10:30
11:00	11:00	11:00	11:00
11:30	11:30	11:30	11:30
12:00	12:00	12:00	12:00
12:30	12:30	12:30	12:30

We are what we repeatedly do... Excellence, then is NOT an act, but a HABIT!	MON	TUES	WED	THURS	FRI	SAT	SUN
10 *BEFORE* 10 GRATITUDE							
DECLARATIONS							
AUDIO							
READ							
FITNESS							
CONTACT 5 *BY* 5							

THOUGHTS / IDEAS / VISIONS / DREAMS

THIS WEEK'S GOAL / FOCUS

WHAT DO I NEED TO...

STOP _____

_____

START _____

_____

CONTINUE _____

_____

_____

QUOTE OF THE WEEK

"Death is not the greatest loss in life. The greatest loss is what dies inside while still alive. Never surrender."

TUPAC AMARU SHAKUR

DECLARATION OF THE WEEK

I am a go-getter, and will go after all my goals and dreams until they are completed.

WRITE YOUR OWN DECLARATIONS FOR THIS WEEK BELOW:

_____
_____
_____
_____
_____
_____
_____
_____
_____
_____
_____
_____
_____
_____
_____
_____
_____
_____

MAXIMIZE YOUR LIFE PLANNER

MAKE IT HAPPEN **MONDAY** ☐	TAKE ACTION **TUESDAY** ☐	WHATEVER IT TAKES **WEDNESDAY** ☐
TODAY'S GOAL	TODAY'S GOAL	TODAY'S GOAL
5:00	5:00	5:00
5:30	5:30	5:30
6:00	6:00	6:00
6:30	6:30	6:30
7:00	7:00	7:00
7:30	7:30	7:30
8:00	8:00	8:00
8:30	8:30	8:30
9:00	9:00	9:00
9:30	9:30	9:30
10:00	10:00	10:00
10:30	10:30	10:30
11:00	11:00	11:00
11:30	11:30	11:30
12:00	12:00	12:00
12:30	12:30	12:30
1:00	1:00	1:00
1:30	1:30	1:30
2:00	2:00	2:00
2:30	2:30	2:30
3:00	3:00	3:00
3:30	3:30	3:30
4:00	4:00	4:00
4:30	4:30	4:30
5:00	5:00	5:00
5:30	5:30	5:30
6:00	6:00	6:00
6:30	6:30	6:30
7:00	7:00	7:00
7:30	7:30	7:30
8:00	8:00	8:00
8:30	8:30	8:30
9:00	9:00	9:00
9:30	9:30	9:30
10:00	10:00	10:00
10:30	10:30	10:30
11:00	11:00	11:00
11:30	11:30	11:30
12:00	12:00	12:00
12:30	12:30	12:30
PERSONAL TO-DO LIST	**WORK** TO-DO LIST	**FOLLOW UP** LIST
☐	☐	/
☐	☐	/
☐	☐	/
☐	☐	/
☐	☐	/
☐	☐	/
☐	☐	/
☐	☐	/
☐	☐	/

TURN IT UP **THURSDAY** ☐	FINISH STRONG **FRIDAY** ☐	STEP IT UP **SATURDAY** ☐	SOULFUL **SUNDAY** ☐
TODAY'S GOAL	TODAY'S GOAL	TODAY'S GOAL	TODAY'S GOAL

THURSDAY	FRIDAY	SATURDAY	SUNDAY
5:00	5:00	5:00	5:00
5:30	5:30	5:30	5:30
6:00	6:00	6:00	6:00
6:30	6:30	6:30	6:30
7:00	7:00	7:00	7:00
7:30	7:30	7:30	7:30
8:00	8:00	8:00	8:00
8:30	8:30	8:30	8:30
9:00	9:00	9:00	9:00
9:30	9:30	9:30	9:30
10:00	10:00	10:00	10:00
10:30	10:30	10:30	10:30
11:00	11:00	11:00	11:00
11:30	11:30	11:30	11:30
12:00	12:00	12:00	12:00
12:30	12:30	12:30	12:30
1:00	1:00	1:00	1:00
1:30	1:30	1:30	1:30
2:00	2:00	2:00	2:00
2:30	2:30	2:30	2:30
3:00	3:00	3:00	3:00
3:30	3:30	3:30	3:30
4:00	4:00	4:00	4:00
4:30	4:30	4:30	4:30
5:00	5:00	5:00	5:00
5:30	5:30	5:30	5:30
6:00	6:00	6:00	6:00
6:30	6:30	6:30	6:30
7:00	7:00	7:00	7:00
7:30	7:30	7:30	7:30
8:00	8:00	8:00	8:00
8:30	8:30	8:30	8:30
9:00	9:00	9:00	9:00
9:30	9:30	9:30	9:30
10:00	10:00	10:00	10:00
10:30	10:30	10:30	10:30
11:00	11:00	11:00	11:00
11:30	11:30	11:30	11:30
12:00	12:00	12:00	12:00
12:30	12:30	12:30	12:30

We are what we repeatedly do... Excellence, then is NOT an act, but a HABIT!	MON	TUES	WED	THURS	FRI	SAT	SUN
10 *BEFORE* 10 GRATITUDE							
DECLARATIONS							
AUDIO							
READ							
FITNESS							
CONTACT 5 *BY* 5							

THOUGHTS / IDEAS / VISIONS / DREAMS

WEEK OF
/ / - / /

THIS WEEK'S GOAL / FOCUS

WHAT DO I NEED TO...

STOP _____

_____

START _____

_____

CONTINUE _____

_____

QUOTE OF THE WEEK
"Do not let making a living prevent you from making a life."
JOHN WOODEN

DECLARATION OF THE WEEK
I have a healthy body, tranquil mind, and vibrant soul.

WRITE YOUR OWN DECLARATIONS FOR THIS WEEK BELOW:

_____
_____
_____
_____
_____
_____
_____
_____
_____
_____
_____
_____
_____
_____
_____
_____

MAXIMIZE
YOUR LIFE
P L A N N E R

MAKE IT HAPPEN **MONDAY** ☐	TAKE ACTION **TUESDAY** ☐	WHATEVER IT TAKES **WEDNESDAY** ☐
TODAY'S GOAL	TODAY'S GOAL	TODAY'S GOAL
5:00	5:00	5:00
5:30	5:30	5:30
6:00	6:00	6:00
6:30	6:30	6:30
7:00	7:00	7:00
7:30	7:30	7:30
8:00	8:00	8:00
8:30	8:30	8:30
9:00	9:00	9:00
9:30	9:30	9:30
10:00	10:00	10:00
10:30	10:30	10:30
11:00	11:00	11:00
11:30	11:30	11:30
12:00	12:00	12:00
12:30	12:30	12:30
1:00	1:00	1:00
1:30	1:30	1:30
2:00	2:00	2:00
2:30	2:30	2:30
3:00	3:00	3:00
3:30	3:30	3:30
4:00	4:00	4:00
4:30	4:30	4:30
5:00	5:00	5:00
5:30	5:30	5:30
6:00	6:00	6:00
6:30	6:30	6:30
7:00	7:00	7:00
7:30	7:30	7:30
8:00	8:00	8:00
8:30	8:30	8:30
9:00	9:00	9:00
9:30	9:30	9:30
10:00	10:00	10:00
10:30	10:30	10:30
11:00	11:00	11:00
11:30	11:30	11:30
12:00	12:00	12:00
12:30	12:30	12:30
PERSONAL TO-DO LIST	**WORK** TO-DO LIST	**FOLLOW UP** LIST
☐	☐	/
☐	☐	/
☐	☐	/
☐	☐	/
☐	☐	/
☐	☐	/
☐	☐	/
☐	☐	/
☐	☐	/

THURSDAY TODAY'S GOAL	FRIDAY TODAY'S GOAL	SATURDAY TODAY'S GOAL	SUNDAY TODAY'S GOAL
5:00	5:00	5:00	5:00
5:30	5:30	5:30	5:30
6:00	6:00	6:00	6:00
6:30	6:30	6:30	6:30
7:00	7:00	7:00	7:00
7:30	7:30	7:30	7:30
8:00	8:00	8:00	8:00
8:30	8:30	8:30	8:30
9:00	9:00	9:00	9:00
9:30	9:30	9:30	9:30
10:00	10:00	10:00	10:00
10:30	10:30	10:30	10:30
11:00	11:00	11:00	11:00
11:30	11:30	11:30	11:30
12:00	12:00	12:00	12:00
12:30	12:30	12:30	12:30
1:00	1:00	1:00	1:00
1:30	1:30	1:30	1:30
2:00	2:00	2:00	2:00
2:30	2:30	2:30	2:30
3:00	3:00	3:00	3:00
3:30	3:30	3:30	3:30
4:00	4:00	4:00	4:00
4:30	4:30	4:30	4:30
5:00	5:00	5:00	5:00
5:30	5:30	5:30	5:30
6:00	6:00	6:00	6:00
6:30	6:30	6:30	6:30
7:00	7:00	7:00	7:00
7:30	7:30	7:30	7:30
8:00	8:00	8:00	8:00
8:30	8:30	8:30	8:30
9:00	9:00	9:00	9:00
9:30	9:30	9:30	9:30
10:00	10:00	10:00	10:00
10:30	10:30	10:30	10:30
11:00	11:00	11:00	11:00
11:30	11:30	11:30	11:30
12:00	12:00	12:00	12:00
12:30	12:30	12:30	12:30

We are what we repeatedly do... Excellence, then is NOT an act, but a HABIT!	MON	TUES	WED	THURS	FRI	SAT	SUN
10 *BEFORE* **10 GRATITUDE**							
DECLARATIONS							
AUDIO							
READ							
FITNESS							
CONTACT 5 *BY* **5**							

THOUGHTS / IDEAS / VISIONS / DREAMS

THIS WEEK'S GOAL / FOCUS

WHAT DO I NEED TO...

STOP _____

_____

START _____

_____

CONTINUE _____

_____

QUOTE OF THE WEEK

*"Love the life you live.
Live the life you love."*
BOB MARLEY

DECLARATION OF THE WEEK

*I possess the qualities needed
to be extremely successful.*

WRITE YOUR OWN DECLARATIONS FOR THIS WEEK BELOW:

_____
_____
_____
_____
_____
_____
_____
_____
_____
_____
_____
_____
_____
_____
_____
_____
_____
_____

MAXIMIZE YOUR LIFE PLANNER

MAKE IT HAPPEN MONDAY ☐	*TAKE ACTION* TUESDAY ☐	*WHATEVER IT TAKES* WEDNESDAY ☐
TODAY'S GOAL	TODAY'S GOAL	TODAY'S GOAL
5:00	5:00	5:00
5:30	5:30	5:30
6:00	6:00	6:00
6:30	6:30	6:30
7:00	7:00	7:00
7:30	7:30	7:30
8:00	8:00	8:00
8:30	8:30	8:30
9:00	9:00	9:00
9:30	9:30	9:30
10:00	10:00	10:00
10:30	10:30	10:30
11:00	11:00	11:00
11:30	11:30	11:30
12:00	12:00	12:00
12:30	12:30	12:30
1:00	1:00	1:00
1:30	1:30	1:30
2:00	2:00	2:00
2:30	2:30	2:30
3:00	3:00	3:00
3:30	3:30	3:30
4:00	4:00	4:00
4:30	4:30	4:30
5:00	5:00	5:00
5:30	5:30	5:30
6:00	6:00	6:00
6:30	6:30	6:30
7:00	7:00	7:00
7:30	7:30	7:30
8:00	8:00	8:00
8:30	8:30	8:30
9:00	9:00	9:00
9:30	9:30	9:30
10:00	10:00	10:00
10:30	10:30	10:30
11:00	11:00	11:00
11:30	11:30	11:30
12:00	12:00	12:00
12:30	12:30	12:30

PERSONAL TO-DO LIST	WORK TO-DO LIST	FOLLOW UP LIST
☐	☐	/
☐	☐	/
☐	☐	/
☐	☐	/
☐	☐	/
☐	☐	/
☐	☐	/
☐	☐	/
☐	☐	/

TODAY'S GOAL	TODAY'S GOAL	TODAY'S GOAL	TODAY'S GOAL
5:00	5:00	5:00	5:00
5:30	5:30	5:30	5:30
6:00	6:00	6:00	6:00
6:30	6:30	6:30	6:30
7:00	7:00	7:00	7:00
7:30	7:30	7:30	7:30
8:00	8:00	8:00	8:00
8:30	8:30	8:30	8:30
9:00	9:00	9:00	9:00
9:30	9:30	9:30	9:30
10:00	10:00	10:00	10:00
10:30	10:30	10:30	10:30
11:00	11:00	11:00	11:00
11:30	11:30	11:30	11:30
12:00	12:00	12:00	12:00
12:30	12:30	12:30	12:30
1:00	1:00	1:00	1:00
1:30	1:30	1:30	1:30
2:00	2:00	2:00	2:00
2:30	2:30	2:30	2:30
3:00	3:00	3:00	3:00
3:30	3:30	3:30	3:30
4:00	4:00	4:00	4:00
4:30	4:30	4:30	4:30
5:00	5:00	5:00	5:00
5:30	5:30	5:30	5:30
6:00	6:00	6:00	6:00
6:30	6:30	6:30	6:30
7:00	7:00	7:00	7:00
7:30	7:30	7:30	7:30
8:00	8:00	8:00	8:00
8:30	8:30	8:30	8:30
9:00	9:00	9:00	9:00
9:30	9:30	9:30	9:30
10:00	10:00	10:00	10:00
10:30	10:30	10:30	10:30
11:00	11:00	11:00	11:00
11:30	11:30	11:30	11:30
12:00	12:00	12:00	12:00
12:30	12:30	12:30	12:30

We are what we repeatedly do... Excellence, then is NOT an act, but a HABIT!	MON	TUES	WED	THURS	FRI	SAT	SUN
10 *BEFORE* 10 GRATITUDE							
DECLARATIONS							
AUDIO							
READ							
FITNESS							
CONTACT 5 *BY* 5							

THOUGHTS / IDEAS / VISIONS / DREAMS

WEEK OF
/ / - / /

THIS WEEK'S GOAL / FOCUS

WHAT DO I NEED TO...

STOP _____

_____

START _____

_____

CONTINUE _____

_____

QUOTE OF THE WEEK

"All our dreams can come true, if we have the courage to pursue them."
WALT DISNEY

DECLARATION OF THE WEEK

I bring happiness and wealth to millions of people in need.

WRITE YOUR OWN DECLARATIONS FOR THIS WEEK BELOW:

_____
_____
_____
_____
_____
_____
_____
_____
_____
_____
_____
_____
_____
_____
_____
_____
_____
_____
_____
_____

MAXIMIZE YOUR LIFE
P L A N N E R

MAKE IT HAPPEN **MONDAY** ☐	*TAKE ACTION* **TUESDAY** ☐	*WHATEVER IT TAKES* **WEDNESDAY** ☐
TODAY'S GOAL	TODAY'S GOAL	TODAY'S GOAL
5:00	5:00	5:00
5:30	5:30	5:30
6:00	6:00	6:00
6:30	6:30	6:30
7:00	7:00	7:00
7:30	7:30	7:30
8:00	8:00	8:00
8:30	8:30	8:30
9:00	9:00	9:00
9:30	9:30	9:30
10:00	10:00	10:00
10:30	10:30	10:30
11:00	11:00	11:00
11:30	11:30	11:30
12:00	12:00	12:00
12:30	12:30	12:30
1:00	1:00	1:00
1:30	1:30	1:30
2:00	2:00	2:00
2:30	2:30	2:30
3:00	3:00	3:00
3:30	3:30	3:30
4:00	4:00	4:00
4:30	4:30	4:30
5:00	5:00	5:00
5:30	5:30	5:30
6:00	6:00	6:00
6:30	6:30	6:30
7:00	7:00	7:00
7:30	7:30	7:30
8:00	8:00	8:00
8:30	8:30	8:30
9:00	9:00	9:00
9:30	9:30	9:30
10:00	10:00	10:00
10:30	10:30	10:30
11:00	11:00	11:00
11:30	11:30	11:30
12:00	12:00	12:00
12:30	12:30	12:30
PERSONAL TO-DO LIST	**WORK** TO-DO LIST	**FOLLOW UP** LIST
☐	☐	/
☐	☐	/
☐	☐	/
☐	☐	/
☐	☐	/
☐	☐	/
☐	☐	/
☐	☐	/
☐	☐	/

TURN IT UP
THURSDAY ☐

FINISH STRONG
FRIDAY ☐

STEP IT UP
SATURDAY ☐

SOULFUL
SUNDAY ☐

TODAY'S GOAL	TODAY'S GOAL	TODAY'S GOAL	TODAY'S GOAL
5:00	5:00	5:00	5:00
5:30	5:30	5:30	5:30
6:00	6:00	6:00	6:00
6:30	6:30	6:30	6:30
7:00	7:00	7:00	7:00
7:30	7:30	7:30	7:30
8:00	8:00	8:00	8:00
8:30	8:30	8:30	8:30
9:00	9:00	9:00	9:00
9:30	9:30	9:30	9:30
10:00	10:00	10:00	10:00
10:30	10:30	10:30	10:30
11:00	11:00	11:00	11:00
11:30	11:30	11:30	11:30
12:00	12:00	12:00	12:00
12:30	12:30	12:30	12:30
1:00	1:00	1:00	1:00
1:30	1:30	1:30	1:30
2:00	2:00	2:00	2:00
2:30	2:30	2:30	2:30
3:00	3:00	3:00	3:00
3:30	3:30	3:30	3:30
4:00	4:00	4:00	4:00
4:30	4:30	4:30	4:30
5:00	5:00	5:00	5:00
5:30	5:30	5:30	5:30
6:00	6:00	6:00	6:00
6:30	6:30	6:30	6:30
7:00	7:00	7:00	7:00
7:30	7:30	7:30	7:30
8:00	8:00	8:00	8:00
8:30	8:30	8:30	8:30
9:00	9:00	9:00	9:00
9:30	9:30	9:30	9:30
10:00	10:00	10:00	10:00
10:30	10:30	10:30	10:30
11:00	11:00	11:00	11:00
11:30	11:30	11:30	11:30
12:00	12:00	12:00	12:00
12:30	12:30	12:30	12:30

We are what we repeatedly do... Excellence, then is NOT an act, but a HABIT!	MON	TUES	WED	THURS	FRI	SAT	SUN
10 *BEFORE* **10 GRATITUDE**							
DECLARATIONS							
AUDIO							
READ							
FITNESS							
CONTACT 5 *BY* **5**							

THOUGHTS / IDEAS / VISIONS / DREAMS

WEEK OF
/ / - / /

THIS WEEK'S GOAL / FOCUS

WHAT DO I NEED TO...

STOP _____
_____

START _____
_____

CONTINUE _____
_____

QUOTE OF THE WEEK
*"Your talent is God's gift to you.
What you do with it is
your gift back to God."*
LEO BUSCAGLIA

DECLARATION OF THE WEEK
*I am filled with gratitude for
another day on this beautiful earth.*

WRITE YOUR OWN
DECLARATIONS FOR
THIS WEEK BELOW:

_____
_____
_____
_____
_____
_____
_____
_____
_____
_____
_____
_____
_____
_____
_____
_____

MAXIMIZE
YOUR LIFE
P L A N N E R

MAKE IT HAPPEN **MONDAY** ☐	*TAKE ACTION* **TUESDAY** ☐	*WHATEVER IT TAKES* **WEDNESDAY** ☐
TODAY'S GOAL	TODAY'S GOAL	TODAY'S GOAL
5:00	5:00	5:00
5:30	5:30	5:30
6:00	6:00	6:00
6:30	6:30	6:30
7:00	7:00	7:00
7:30	7:30	7:30
8:00	8:00	8:00
8:30	8:30	8:30
9:00	9:00	9:00
9:30	9:30	9:30
10:00	10:00	10:00
10:30	10:30	10:30
11:00	11:00	11:00
11:30	11:30	11:30
12:00	12:00	12:00
12:30	12:30	12:30
1:00	1:00	1:00
1:30	1:30	1:30
2:00	2:00	2:00
2:30	2:30	2:30
3:00	3:00	3:00
3:30	3:30	3:30
4:00	4:00	4:00
4:30	4:30	4:30
5:00	5:00	5:00
5:30	5:30	5:30
6:00	6:00	6:00
6:30	6:30	6:30
7:00	7:00	7:00
7:30	7:30	7:30
8:00	8:00	8:00
8:30	8:30	8:30
9:00	9:00	9:00
9:30	9:30	9:30
10:00	10:00	10:00
10:30	10:30	10:30
11:00	11:00	11:00
11:30	11:30	11:30
12:00	12:00	12:00
12:30	12:30	12:30
PERSONAL TO-DO LIST	**WORK** TO-DO LIST	**FOLLOW UP** LIST
☐	☐	/
☐	☐	/
☐	☐	/
☐	☐	/
☐	☐	/
☐	☐	/
☐	☐	/
☐	☐	/
☐	☐	/

TODAY'S GOAL (THURSDAY) | **TODAY'S GOAL** (FRIDAY) | **TODAY'S GOAL** (SATURDAY) | **TODAY'S GOAL** (SUNDAY)

THURSDAY	FRIDAY	SATURDAY	SUNDAY
5:00	5:00	5:00	5:00
5:30	5:30	5:30	5:30
6:00	6:00	6:00	6:00
6:30	6:30	6:30	6:30
7:00	7:00	7:00	7:00
7:30	7:30	7:30	7:30
8:00	8:00	8:00	8:00
8:30	8:30	8:30	8:30
9:00	9:00	9:00	9:00
9:30	9:30	9:30	9:30
10:00	10:00	10:00	10:00
10:30	10:30	10:30	10:30
11:00	11:00	11:00	11:00
11:30	11:30	11:30	11:30
12:00	12:00	12:00	12:00
12:30	12:30	12:30	12:30
1:00	1:00	1:00	1:00
1:30	1:30	1:30	1:30
2:00	2:00	2:00	2:00
2:30	2:30	2:30	2:30
3:00	3:00	3:00	3:00
3:30	3:30	3:30	3:30
4:00	4:00	4:00	4:00
4:30	4:30	4:30	4:30
5:00	5:00	5:00	5:00
5:30	5:30	5:30	5:30
6:00	6:00	6:00	6:00
6:30	6:30	6:30	6:30
7:00	7:00	7:00	7:00
7:30	7:30	7:30	7:30
8:00	8:00	8:00	8:00
8:30	8:30	8:30	8:30
9:00	9:00	9:00	9:00
9:30	9:30	9:30	9:30
10:00	10:00	10:00	10:00
10:30	10:30	10:30	10:30
11:00	11:00	11:00	11:00
11:30	11:30	11:30	11:30
12:00	12:00	12:00	12:00
12:30	12:30	12:30	12:30

We are what we repeatedly do... Excellence, then is NOT an act, but a HABIT!

	MON	TUES	WED	THURS	FRI	SAT	SUN
10 BEFORE 10 GRATITUDE							
DECLARATIONS							
AUDIO							
READ							
FITNESS							
CONTACT 5 BY 5							

THOUGHTS / IDEAS / VISIONS / DREAMS

WEEK OF
/ / - / /

THIS WEEK'S GOAL / FOCUS

WHAT DO I NEED TO...

STOP _____
_____

START _____
_____

CONTINUE _____
_____

QUOTE OF THE WEEK

"Your purpose in life is to discover your God-given genius and utilize it to make a positive impact on the world around you."
MAXIMO LORA

DECLARATION OF THE WEEK

I am so happy and grateful now that I have earned more income than ever before, as I empower people around the world to reach their higher self while living an abundant lifestyle.

WRITE YOUR OWN DECLARATIONS FOR THIS WEEK BELOW:

_____
_____
_____
_____
_____
_____
_____
_____
_____
_____
_____
_____
_____
_____
_____
_____

MAXIMIZE YOUR LIFE PLANNER

	MAKE IT HAPPEN MONDAY ☐	TAKE ACTION TUESDAY ☐	WHATEVER IT TAKES WEDNESDAY ☐
	TODAY'S GOAL	TODAY'S GOAL	TODAY'S GOAL
5:00			
5:30			
6:00			
6:30			
7:00			
7:30			
8:00			
8:30			
9:00			
9:30			
10:00			
10:30			
11:00			
11:30			
12:00			
12:30			
1:00			
1:30			
2:00			
2:30			
3:00			
3:30			
4:00			
4:30			
5:00			
5:30			
6:00			
6:30			
7:00			
7:30			
8:00			
8:30			
9:00			
9:30			
10:00			
10:30			
11:00			
11:30			
12:00			
12:30			

PERSONAL TO-DO LIST	WORK TO-DO LIST	FOLLOW UP LIST
☐	☐	/
☐	☐	/
☐	☐	/
☐	☐	/
☐	☐	/
☐	☐	/
☐	☐	/
☐	☐	/
☐	☐	/

TODAY'S GOAL	TODAY'S GOAL	TODAY'S GOAL	TODAY'S GOAL
5:00	5:00	5:00	5:00
5:30	5:30	5:30	5:30
6:00	6:00	6:00	6:00
6:30	6:30	6:30	6:30
7:00	7:00	7:00	7:00
7:30	7:30	7:30	7:30
8:00	8:00	8:00	8:00
8:30	8:30	8:30	8:30
9:00	9:00	9:00	9:00
9:30	9:30	9:30	9:30
10:00	10:00	10:00	10:00
10:30	10:30	10:30	10:30
11:00	11:00	11:00	11:00
11:30	11:30	11:30	11:30
12:00	12:00	12:00	12:00
12:30	12:30	12:30	12:30
1:00	1:00	1:00	1:00
1:30	1:30	1:30	1:30
2:00	2:00	2:00	2:00
2:30	2:30	2:30	2:30
3:00	3:00	3:00	3:00
3:30	3:30	3:30	3:30
4:00	4:00	4:00	4:00
4:30	4:30	4:30	4:30
5:00	5:00	5:00	5:00
5:30	5:30	5:30	5:30
6:00	6:00	6:00	6:00
6:30	6:30	6:30	6:30
7:00	7:00	7:00	7:00
7:30	7:30	7:30	7:30
8:00	8:00	8:00	8:00
8:30	8:30	8:30	8:30
9:00	9:00	9:00	9:00
9:30	9:30	9:30	9:30
10:00	10:00	10:00	10:00
10:30	10:30	10:30	10:30
11:00	11:00	11:00	11:00
11:30	11:30	11:30	11:30
12:00	12:00	12:00	12:00
12:30	12:30	12:30	12:30

We are what we repeatedly do... Excellence, then is NOT an act, but a HABIT!	MON	TUES	WED	THURS	FRI	SAT	SUN
10 BEFORE 10 GRATITUDE							
DECLARATIONS							
AUDIO							
READ							
FITNESS							
CONTACT 5 BY 5							

THOUGHTS / IDEAS / VISIONS / DREAMS

WEEK OF / / - / /

THIS WEEK'S GOAL / FOCUS

WHAT DO I NEED TO...

STOP _____

_____

START _____

_____

CONTINUE _____

_____

_____

QUOTE OF THE WEEK

"Successful people do what unsuccessful people are not willing to do. Don't wish it were easier, wish you were better."
JIM ROHN

DECLARATION OF THE WEEK

I have a wonderful opportunity in a wonderful way. I give wonderful value for wonderful pay!

WRITE YOUR OWN DECLARATIONS FOR THIS WEEK BELOW:

_____
_____
_____
_____
_____
_____
_____
_____
_____
_____
_____
_____
_____
_____
_____
_____
_____

MAXIMIZE YOUR LIFE PLANNER

MAKE IT HAPPEN MONDAY ☐	*TAKE ACTION* TUESDAY ☐	*WHATEVER IT TAKES* WEDNESDAY ☐
TODAY'S GOAL	TODAY'S GOAL	TODAY'S GOAL
5:00	5:00	5:00
5:30	5:30	5:30
6:00	6:00	6:00
6:30	6:30	6:30
7:00	7:00	7:00
7:30	7:30	7:30
8:00	8:00	8:00
8:30	8:30	8:30
9:00	9:00	9:00
9:30	9:30	9:30
10:00	10:00	10:00
10:30	10:30	10:30
11:00	11:00	11:00
11:30	11:30	11:30
12:00	12:00	12:00
12:30	12:30	12:30
1:00	1:00	1:00
1:30	1:30	1:30
2:00	2:00	2:00
2:30	2:30	2:30
3:00	3:00	3:00
3:30	3:30	3:30
4:00	4:00	4:00
4:30	4:30	4:30
5:00	5:00	5:00
5:30	5:30	5:30
6:00	6:00	6:00
6:30	6:30	6:30
7:00	7:00	7:00
7:30	7:30	7:30
8:00	8:00	8:00
8:30	8:30	8:30
9:00	9:00	9:00
9:30	9:30	9:30
10:00	10:00	10:00
10:30	10:30	10:30
11:00	11:00	11:00
11:30	11:30	11:30
12:00	12:00	12:00
12:30	12:30	12:30
PERSONAL TO-DO LIST	**WORK** TO-DO LIST	**FOLLOW UP** LIST
☐	☐	/
☐	☐	/
☐	☐	/
☐	☐	/
☐	☐	/
☐	☐	/
☐	☐	/
☐	☐	/
☐	☐	/

TURN IT UP
THURSDAY ☐

FINISH STRONG
FRIDAY ☐

STEP IT UP
SATURDAY ☐

SOULFUL
SUNDAY ☐

TODAY'S GOAL	TODAY'S GOAL	TODAY'S GOAL	TODAY'S GOAL
5:00	5:00	5:00	5:00
5:30	5:30	5:30	5:30
6:00	6:00	6:00	6:00
6:30	6:30	6:30	6:30
7:00	7:00	7:00	7:00
7:30	7:30	7:30	7:30
8:00	8:00	8:00	8:00
8:30	8:30	8:30	8:30
9:00	9:00	9:00	9:00
9:30	9:30	9:30	9:30
10:00	10:00	10:00	10:00
10:30	10:30	10:30	10:30
11:00	11:00	11:00	11:00
11:30	11:30	11:30	11:30
12:00	12:00	12:00	12:00
12:30	12:30	12:30	12:30
1:00	1:00	1:00	1:00
1:30	1:30	1:30	1:30
2:00	2:00	2:00	2:00
2:30	2:30	2:30	2:30
3:00	3:00	3:00	3:00
3:30	3:30	3:30	3:30
4:00	4:00	4:00	4:00
4:30	4:30	4:30	4:30
5:00	5:00	5:00	5:00
5:30	5:30	5:30	5:30
6:00	6:00	6:00	6:00
6:30	6:30	6:30	6:30
7:00	7:00	7:00	7:00
7:30	7:30	7:30	7:30
8:00	8:00	8:00	8:00
8:30	8:30	8:30	8:30
9:00	9:00	9:00	9:00
9:30	9:30	9:30	9:30
10:00	10:00	10:00	10:00
10:30	10:30	10:30	10:30
11:00	11:00	11:00	11:00
11:30	11:30	11:30	11:30
12:00	12:00	12:00	12:00
12:30	12:30	12:30	12:30

We are what we repeatedly do... Excellence, then is NOT an act, but a HABIT!	MON	TUES	WED	THURS	FRI	SAT	SUN
10 *BEFORE* **10 GRATITUDE**							
DECLARATIONS							
AUDIO							
READ							
FITNESS							
CONTACT 5 *BY* **5**							

THOUGHTS / IDEAS / VISIONS / DREAMS

THIS WEEK'S GOAL / FOCUS

WHAT DO I NEED TO...

STOP _____

_____

START _____

_____

CONTINUE _____

_____

QUOTE OF THE WEEK

"You miss 100% of the shots you don't take."
WAYNE GRETZKY

DECLARATION OF THE WEEK

I have an amazing relationship with my partner that gets stronger, deeper, and more stable each and every day.

WRITE YOUR OWN DECLARATIONS FOR THIS WEEK BELOW:

MAKE IT HAPPEN **MONDAY** ☐	TAKE ACTION **TUESDAY** ☐	WHATEVER IT TAKES **WEDNESDAY** ☐
TODAY'S GOAL	TODAY'S GOAL	TODAY'S GOAL
5:00	5:00	5:00
5:30	5:30	5:30
6:00	6:00	6:00
6:30	6:30	6:30
7:00	7:00	7:00
7:30	7:30	7:30
8:00	8:00	8:00
8:30	8:30	8:30
9:00	9:00	9:00
9:30	9:30	9:30
10:00	10:00	10:00
10:30	10:30	10:30
11:00	11:00	11:00
11:30	11:30	11:30
12:00	12:00	12:00
12:30	12:30	12:30
1:00	1:00	1:00
1:30	1:30	1:30
2:00	2:00	2:00
2:30	2:30	2:30
3:00	3:00	3:00
3:30	3:30	3:30
4:00	4:00	4:00
4:30	4:30	4:30
5:00	5:00	5:00
5:30	5:30	5:30
6:00	6:00	6:00
6:30	6:30	6:30
7:00	7:00	7:00
7:30	7:30	7:30
8:00	8:00	8:00
8:30	8:30	8:30
9:00	9:00	9:00
9:30	9:30	9:30
10:00	10:00	10:00
10:30	10:30	10:30
11:00	11:00	11:00
11:30	11:30	11:30
12:00	12:00	12:00
12:30	12:30	12:30
PERSONAL TO-DO LIST	**WORK** TO-DO LIST	**FOLLOW UP** LIST
☐	☐	/
☐	☐	/
☐	☐	/
☐	☐	/
☐	☐	/
☐	☐	/
☐	☐	/
☐	☐	/
☐	☐	/
☐	☐	/

MAXIMIZE YOUR LIFE
P L A N N E R

TURN IT UP **THURSDAY** ☐	FINISH STRONG **FRIDAY** ☐	STEP IT UP **SATURDAY** ☐	SOULFUL **SUNDAY** ☐
TODAY'S GOAL	TODAY'S GOAL	TODAY'S GOAL	TODAY'S GOAL

Thursday	Friday	Saturday	Sunday
5:00	5:00	5:00	5:00
5:30	5:30	5:30	5:30
6:00	6:00	6:00	6:00
6:30	6:30	6:30	6:30
7:00	7:00	7:00	7:00
7:30	7:30	7:30	7:30
8:00	8:00	8:00	8:00
8:30	8:30	8:30	8:30
9:00	9:00	9:00	9:00
9:30	9:30	9:30	9:30
10:00	10:00	10:00	10:00
10:30	10:30	10:30	10:30
11:00	11:00	11:00	11:00
11:30	11:30	11:30	11:30
12:00	12:00	12:00	12:00
12:30	12:30	12:30	12:30
1:00	1:00	1:00	1:00
1:30	1:30	1:30	1:30
2:00	2:00	2:00	2:00
2:30	2:30	2:30	2:30
3:00	3:00	3:00	3:00
3:30	3:30	3:30	3:30
4:00	4:00	4:00	4:00
4:30	4:30	4:30	4:30
5:00	5:00	5:00	5:00
5:30	5:30	5:30	5:30
6:00	6:00	6:00	6:00
6:30	6:30	6:30	6:30
7:00	7:00	7:00	7:00
7:30	7:30	7:30	7:30
8:00	8:00	8:00	8:00
8:30	8:30	8:30	8:30
9:00	9:00	9:00	9:00
9:30	9:30	9:30	9:30
10:00	10:00	10:00	10:00
10:30	10:30	10:30	10:30
11:00	11:00	11:00	11:00
11:30	11:30	11:30	11:30
12:00	12:00	12:00	12:00
12:30	12:30	12:30	12:30

We are what we repeatedly do... Excellence, then is NOT an act, but a HABIT!	MON	TUES	WED	THURS	FRI	SAT	SUN
10 *BEFORE* 10 GRATITUDE							
DECLARATIONS							
AUDIO							
READ							
FITNESS							
CONTACT 5 *BY* 5							

THOUGHTS / IDEAS / VISIONS / DREAMS

THIS WEEK'S GOAL / FOCUS

WHAT DO I NEED TO...

STOP _____

_____

START _____

_____

CONTINUE _____

_____

QUOTE OF THE WEEK

"Some of God's greatest gifts are unanswered prayers."
GARTH BROOKS

DECLARATION OF THE WEEK

I am supported and loved by God.

WRITE YOUR OWN DECLARATIONS FOR THIS WEEK BELOW:

_____
_____
_____
_____
_____
_____
_____
_____
_____
_____
_____
_____
_____
_____
_____
_____
_____
_____
_____

	TODAY'S GOAL	TODAY'S GOAL	TODAY'S GOAL
5:00			
5:30			
6:00			
6:30			
7:00			
7:30			
8:00			
8:30			
9:00			
9:30			
10:00			
10:30			
11:00			
11:30			
12:00			
12:30			
1:00			
1:30			
2:00			
2:30			
3:00			
3:30			
4:00			
4:30			
5:00			
5:30			
6:00			
6:30			
7:00			
7:30			
8:00			
8:30			
9:00			
9:30			
10:00			
10:30			
11:00			
11:30			
12:00			
12:30			

PERSONAL TO-DO LIST	WORK TO-DO LIST	FOLLOW UP LIST
☐	☐	/
☐	☐	/
☐	☐	/
☐	☐	/
☐	☐	/
☐	☐	/
☐	☐	/
☐	☐	/

MAXIMIZE YOUR LIFE P L A N N E R

TODAY'S GOAL	TODAY'S GOAL	TODAY'S GOAL	TODAY'S GOAL
5:00	5:00	5:00	5:00
5:30	5:30	5:30	5:30
6:00	6:00	6:00	6:00
6:30	6:30	6:30	6:30
7:00	7:00	7:00	7:00
7:30	7:30	7:30	7:30
8:00	8:00	8:00	8:00
8:30	8:30	8:30	8:30
9:00	9:00	9:00	9:00
9:30	9:30	9:30	9:30
10:00	10:00	10:00	10:00
10:30	10:30	10:30	10:30
11:00	11:00	11:00	11:00
11:30	11:30	11:30	11:30
12:00	12:00	12:00	12:00
12:30	12:30	12:30	12:30
1:00	1:00	1:00	1:00
1:30	1:30	1:30	1:30
2:00	2:00	2:00	2:00
2:30	2:30	2:30	2:30
3:00	3:00	3:00	3:00
3:30	3:30	3:30	3:30
4:00	4:00	4:00	4:00
4:30	4:30	4:30	4:30
5:00	5:00	5:00	5:00
5:30	5:30	5:30	5:30
6:00	6:00	6:00	6:00
6:30	6:30	6:30	6:30
7:00	7:00	7:00	7:00
7:30	7:30	7:30	7:30
8:00	8:00	8:00	8:00
8:30	8:30	8:30	8:30
9:00	9:00	9:00	9:00
9:30	9:30	9:30	9:30
10:00	10:00	10:00	10:00
10:30	10:30	10:30	10:30
11:00	11:00	11:00	11:00
11:30	11:30	11:30	11:30
12:00	12:00	12:00	12:00
12:30	12:30	12:30	12:30

We are what we repeatedly do... Excellence, then is NOT an act, but a HABIT!	MON	TUES	WED	THURS	FRI	SAT	SUN
10 BEFORE 10 GRATITUDE							
DECLARATIONS							
AUDIO							
READ							
FITNESS							
CONTACT 5 BY 5							

THOUGHTS / IDEAS / VISIONS / DREAMS

WEEK OF
/ / - / /

THIS WEEK'S GOAL / FOCUS

WHAT DO I NEED TO...

STOP _____
_____

START _____
_____

CONTINUE _____
_____

QUOTE OF THE WEEK
"Whether you think you can or you think you can't, you're right."
HENRY FORD

DECLARATION OF THE WEEK
I am open and willing to receive massive amounts of income into my life.

WRITE YOUR OWN DECLARATIONS FOR THIS WEEK BELOW:
_____
_____
_____
_____
_____
_____
_____
_____
_____
_____
_____
_____

MAXIMIZE YOUR LIFE PLANNER

MAKE IT HAPPEN **MONDAY** ☐	TAKE ACTION **TUESDAY** ☐	WHATEVER IT TAKES **WEDNESDAY** ☐
TODAY'S GOAL	TODAY'S GOAL	TODAY'S GOAL
5:00	5:00	5:00
5:30	5:30	5:30
6:00	6:00	6:00
6:30	6:30	6:30
7:00	7:00	7:00
7:30	7:30	7:30
8:00	8:00	8:00
8:30	8:30	8:30
9:00	9:00	9:00
9:30	9:30	9:30
10:00	10:00	10:00
10:30	10:30	10:30
11:00	11:00	11:00
11:30	11:30	11:30
12:00	12:00	12:00
12:30	12:30	12:30
1:00	1:00	1:00
1:30	1:30	1:30
2:00	2:00	2:00
2:30	2:30	2:30
3:00	3:00	3:00
3:30	3:30	3:30
4:00	4:00	4:00
4:30	4:30	4:30
5:00	5:00	5:00
5:30	5:30	5:30
6:00	6:00	6:00
6:30	6:30	6:30
7:00	7:00	7:00
7:30	7:30	7:30
8:00	8:00	8:00
8:30	8:30	8:30
9:00	9:00	9:00
9:30	9:30	9:30
10:00	10:00	10:00
10:30	10:30	10:30
11:00	11:00	11:00
11:30	11:30	11:30
12:00	12:00	12:00
12:30	12:30	12:30
PERSONAL TO-DO LIST	**WORK** TO-DO LIST	**FOLLOW UP** LIST
☐	☐	/
☐	☐	/
☐	☐	/
☐	☐	/
☐	☐	/
☐	☐	/
☐	☐	/
☐	☐	/
☐	☐	/
☐	☐	/

TURN IT UP
THURSDAY ☐

FINISH STRONG
FRIDAY ☐

STEP IT UP
SATURDAY ☐

SOULFUL
SUNDAY ☐

THURSDAY	FRIDAY	SATURDAY	SUNDAY
TODAY'S GOAL	TODAY'S GOAL	TODAY'S GOAL	TODAY'S GOAL

THURSDAY	FRIDAY	SATURDAY	SUNDAY
5:00	5:00	5:00	5:00
5:30	5:30	5:30	5:30
6:00	6:00	6:00	6:00
6:30	6:30	6:30	6:30
7:00	7:00	7:00	7:00
7:30	7:30	7:30	7:30
8:00	8:00	8:00	8:00
8:30	8:30	8:30	8:30
9:00	9:00	9:00	9:00
9:30	9:30	9:30	9:30
10:00	10:00	10:00	10:00
10:30	10:30	10:30	10:30
11:00	11:00	11:00	11:00
11:30	11:30	11:30	11:30
12:00	12:00	12:00	12:00
12:30	12:30	12:30	12:30
1:00	1:00	1:00	1:00
1:30	1:30	1:30	1:30
2:00	2:00	2:00	2:00
2:30	2:30	2:30	2:30
3:00	3:00	3:00	3:00
3:30	3:30	3:30	3:30
4:00	4:00	4:00	4:00
4:30	4:30	4:30	4:30
5:00	5:00	5:00	5:00
5:30	5:30	5:30	5:30
6:00	6:00	6:00	6:00
6:30	6:30	6:30	6:30
7:00	7:00	7:00	7:00
7:30	7:30	7:30	7:30
8:00	8:00	8:00	8:00
8:30	8:30	8:30	8:30
9:00	9:00	9:00	9:00
9:30	9:30	9:30	9:30
10:00	10:00	10:00	10:00
10:30	10:30	10:30	10:30
11:00	11:00	11:00	11:00
11:30	11:30	11:30	11:30
12:00	12:00	12:00	12:00
12:30	12:30	12:30	12:30

We are what we repeatedly do... Excellence, then is NOT an act, but a HABIT!	MON	TUES	WED	THURS	FRI	SAT	SUN
10 *BEFORE* 10 GRATITUDE							
DECLARATIONS							
AUDIO							
READ							
FITNESS							
CONTACT 5 *BY* 5							

THOUGHTS / IDEAS / VISIONS / DREAMS

THIS WEEK'S GOAL / FOCUS

WHAT DO I NEED TO...

STOP _____

_____

START _____

_____

CONTINUE _____

_____

_____

QUOTE OF THE WEEK

"What God intended for you goes far beyond anything you can imagine."
OPRAH WINFREY

DECLARATION OF THE WEEK

Feels amazing to help our foundation raise large sums of money yearly towards our on-going programming.

WRITE YOUR OWN DECLARATIONS FOR THIS WEEK BELOW:

_____
_____
_____
_____
_____
_____
_____
_____
_____
_____
_____
_____
_____
_____
_____
_____
_____

MAXIMIZE
YOUR LIFE
P L A N N E R

MAKE IT HAPPEN **MONDAY** ☐	TAKE ACTION **TUESDAY** ☐	WHATEVER IT TAKES **WEDNESDAY** ☐
TODAY'S GOAL	TODAY'S GOAL	TODAY'S GOAL
5:00	5:00	5:00
5:30	5:30	5:30
6:00	6:00	6:00
6:30	6:30	6:30
7:00	7:00	7:00
7:30	7:30	7:30
8:00	8:00	8:00
8:30	8:30	8:30
9:00	9:00	9:00
9:30	9:30	9:30
10:00	10:00	10:00
10:30	10:30	10:30
11:00	11:00	11:00
11:30	11:30	11:30
12:00	12:00	12:00
12:30	12:30	12:30
1:00	1:00	1:00
1:30	1:30	1:30
2:00	2:00	2:00
2:30	2:30	2:30
3:00	3:00	3:00
3:30	3:30	3:30
4:00	4:00	4:00
4:30	4:30	4:30
5:00	5:00	5:00
5:30	5:30	5:30
6:00	6:00	6:00
6:30	6:30	6:30
7:00	7:00	7:00
7:30	7:30	7:30
8:00	8:00	8:00
8:30	8:30	8:30
9:00	9:00	9:00
9:30	9:30	9:30
10:00	10:00	10:00
10:30	10:30	10:30
11:00	11:00	11:00
11:30	11:30	11:30
12:00	12:00	12:00
12:30	12:30	12:30
PERSONAL TO-DO LIST	**WORK** TO-DO LIST	**FOLLOW UP** LIST
☐	☐	/
☐	☐	/
☐	☐	/
☐	☐	/
☐	☐	/
☐	☐	/
☐	☐	/
☐	☐	/
☐	☐	/

TURN IT UP		FINISH STRONG		STEP IT UP		SOULFUL	
THURSDAY	☐	**FRIDAY**	☐	**SATURDAY**	☐	**SUNDAY**	☐

TODAY'S GOAL — TODAY'S GOAL — TODAY'S GOAL — TODAY'S GOAL

THURSDAY	FRIDAY	SATURDAY	SUNDAY
5:00	5:00	5:00	5:00
5:30	5:30	5:30	5:30
6:00	6:00	6:00	6:00
6:30	6:30	6:30	6:30
7:00	7:00	7:00	7:00
7:30	7:30	7:30	7:30
8:00	8:00	8:00	8:00
8:30	8:30	8:30	8:30
9:00	9:00	9:00	9:00
9:30	9:30	9:30	9:30
10:00	10:00	10:00	10:00
10:30	10:30	10:30	10:30
11:00	11:00	11:00	11:00
11:30	11:30	11:30	11:30
12:00	12:00	12:00	12:00
12:30	12:30	12:30	12:30
1:00	1:00	1:00	1:00
1:30	1:30	1:30	1:30
2:00	2:00	2:00	2:00
2:30	2:30	2:30	2:30
3:00	3:00	3:00	3:00
3:30	3:30	3:30	3:30
4:00	4:00	4:00	4:00
4:30	4:30	4:30	4:30
5:00	5:00	5:00	5:00
5:30	5:30	5:30	5:30
6:00	6:00	6:00	6:00
6:30	6:30	6:30	6:30
7:00	7:00	7:00	7:00
7:30	7:30	7:30	7:30
8:00	8:00	8:00	8:00
8:30	8:30	8:30	8:30
9:00	9:00	9:00	9:00
9:30	9:30	9:30	9:30
10:00	10:00	10:00	10:00
10:30	10:30	10:30	10:30
11:00	11:00	11:00	11:00
11:30	11:30	11:30	11:30
12:00	12:00	12:00	12:00
12:30	12:30	12:30	12:30

We are what we repeatedly do... Excellence, then is NOT an act, but a HABIT!	MON	TUES	WED	THURS	FRI	SAT	SUN
10 *BEFORE* **10 GRATITUDE**							
DECLARATIONS							
AUDIO							
READ							
FITNESS							
CONTACT 5 *BY* **5**							

THOUGHTS / IDEAS / VISIONS / DREAMS

WEEK OF

/ / - / /

WHAT DO I NEED TO...

STOP _____

_____

START _____

_____

CONTINUE _____

_____

QUOTE OF THE WEEK

"Faith is to believe what you do not see... the reward of this faith is to see what you believe."

SAINT AUGUSTINE

DECLARATION OF THE WEEK

I am constantly growing and improving, both personally and professionally.

WRITE YOUR OWN DECLARATIONS FOR THIS WEEK BELOW:

_____
_____
_____
_____
_____
_____
_____
_____
_____
_____
_____
_____
_____
_____
_____

MAXIMIZE
YOUR LIFE
P L A N N E R

	MAKE IT HAPPEN **MONDAY** ☐	*TAKE ACTION* **TUESDAY** ☐	*WHATEVER IT TAKES* **WEDNESDAY** ☐
	TODAY'S GOAL	TODAY'S GOAL	TODAY'S GOAL
5:00			
5:30			
6:00			
6:30			
7:00			
7:30			
8:00			
8:30			
9:00			
9:30			
10:00			
10:30			
11:00			
11:30			
12:00			
12:30			
1:00			
1:30			
2:00			
2:30			
3:00			
3:30			
4:00			
4:30			
5:00			
5:30			
6:00			
6:30			
7:00			
7:30			
8:00			
8:30			
9:00			
9:30			
10:00			
10:30			
11:00			
11:30			
12:00			
12:30			

PERSONAL TO-DO LIST	**WORK** TO-DO LIST	**FOLLOW UP** LIST
☐	☐	/
☐	☐	/
☐	☐	/
☐	☐	/
☐	☐	/
☐	☐	/
☐	☐	/
☐	☐	/
☐	☐	/

TURN IT UP **THURSDAY** ☐	FINISH STRONG **FRIDAY** ☐	STEP IT UP **SATURDAY** ☐	SOULFUL **SUNDAY** ☐
TODAY'S GOAL	TODAY'S GOAL	TODAY'S GOAL	TODAY'S GOAL

THURSDAY	FRIDAY	SATURDAY	SUNDAY
5:00	5:00	5:00	5:00
5:30	5:30	5:30	5:30
6:00	6:00	6:00	6:00
6:30	6:30	6:30	6:30
7:00	7:00	7:00	7:00
7:30	7:30	7:30	7:30
8:00	8:00	8:00	8:00
8:30	8:30	8:30	8:30
9:00	9:00	9:00	9:00
9:30	9:30	9:30	9:30
10:00	10:00	10:00	10:00
10:30	10:30	10:30	10:30
11:00	11:00	11:00	11:00
11:30	11:30	11:30	11:30
12:00	12:00	12:00	12:00
12:30	12:30	12:30	12:30
1:00	1:00	1:00	1:00
1:30	1:30	1:30	1:30
2:00	2:00	2:00	2:00
2:30	2:30	2:30	2:30
3:00	3:00	3:00	3:00
3:30	3:30	3:30	3:30
4:00	4:00	4:00	4:00
4:30	4:30	4:30	4:30
5:00	5:00	5:00	5:00
5:30	5:30	5:30	5:30
6:00	6:00	6:00	6:00
6:30	6:30	6:30	6:30
7:00	7:00	7:00	7:00
7:30	7:30	7:30	7:30
8:00	8:00	8:00	8:00
8:30	8:30	8:30	8:30
9:00	9:00	9:00	9:00
9:30	9:30	9:30	9:30
10:00	10:00	10:00	10:00
10:30	10:30	10:30	10:30
11:00	11:00	11:00	11:00
11:30	11:30	11:30	11:30
12:00	12:00	12:00	12:00
12:30	12:30	12:30	12:30

We are what we repeatedly do... Excellence, then is NOT an act, but a HABIT!	MON	TUES	WED	THURS	FRI	SAT	SUN
10 *BEFORE* **10 GRATITUDE**							
DECLARATIONS							
AUDIO							
READ							
FITNESS							
CONTACT 5 *BY* **5**							

THOUGHTS / IDEAS / VISIONS / DREAMS

THIS WEEK'S GOAL / FOCUS

WHAT DO I NEED TO...

STOP _____

_____

START _____

_____

CONTINUE _____

_____

_____

QUOTE OF THE WEEK

"In order to write about life first you must live it."
ERNEST HEMINGWAY

DECLARATION OF THE WEEK

I am of a strong heart and steel body. I am vigorous, energetic, and full of vitality.

WRITE YOUR OWN DECLARATIONS FOR THIS WEEK BELOW:

_____
_____
_____
_____
_____
_____
_____
_____
_____
_____
_____
_____
_____
_____
_____
_____
_____
_____
_____

MAXIMIZE YOUR LIFE PLANNER

MAKE IT HAPPEN **MONDAY** ☐	*TAKE ACTION* **TUESDAY** ☐	*WHATEVER IT TAKES* **WEDNESDAY** ☐
TODAY'S GOAL	TODAY'S GOAL	TODAY'S GOAL
5:00	5:00	5:00
5:30	5:30	5:30
6:00	6:00	6:00
6:30	6:30	6:30
7:00	7:00	7:00
7:30	7:30	7:30
8:00	8:00	8:00
8:30	8:30	8:30
9:00	9:00	9:00
9:30	9:30	9:30
10:00	10:00	10:00
10:30	10:30	10:30
11:00	11:00	11:00
11:30	11:30	11:30
12:00	12:00	12:00
12:30	12:30	12:30
1:00	1:00	1:00
1:30	1:30	1:30
2:00	2:00	2:00
2:30	2:30	2:30
3:00	3:00	3:00
3:30	3:30	3:30
4:00	4:00	4:00
4:30	4:30	4:30
5:00	5:00	5:00
5:30	5:30	5:30
6:00	6:00	6:00
6:30	6:30	6:30
7:00	7:00	7:00
7:30	7:30	7:30
8:00	8:00	8:00
8:30	8:30	8:30
9:00	9:00	9:00
9:30	9:30	9:30
10:00	10:00	10:00
10:30	10:30	10:30
11:00	11:00	11:00
11:30	11:30	11:30
12:00	12:00	12:00
12:30	12:30	12:30
PERSONAL TO-DO LIST	**WORK** TO-DO LIST	**FOLLOW UP** LIST
☐	☐	/
☐	☐	/
☐	☐	/
☐	☐	/
☐	☐	/
☐	☐	/
☐	☐	/
☐	☐	/
☐	☐	/

TODAY'S GOAL | TODAY'S GOAL | TODAY'S GOAL | TODAY'S GOAL

THURSDAY	FRIDAY	SATURDAY	SUNDAY
5:00	5:00	5:00	5:00
5:30	5:30	5:30	5:30
6:00	6:00	6:00	6:00
6:30	6:30	6:30	6:30
7:00	7:00	7:00	7:00
7:30	7:30	7:30	7:30
8:00	8:00	8:00	8:00
8:30	8:30	8:30	8:30
9:00	9:00	9:00	9:00
9:30	9:30	9:30	9:30
10:00	10:00	10:00	10:00
10:30	10:30	10:30	10:30
11:00	11:00	11:00	11:00
11:30	11:30	11:30	11:30
12:00	12:00	12:00	12:00
12:30	12:30	12:30	12:30
1:00	1:00	1:00	1:00
1:30	1:30	1:30	1:30
2:00	2:00	2:00	2:00
2:30	2:30	2:30	2:30
3:00	3:00	3:00	3:00
3:30	3:30	3:30	3:30
4:00	4:00	4:00	4:00
4:30	4:30	4:30	4:30
5:00	5:00	5:00	5:00
5:30	5:30	5:30	5:30
6:00	6:00	6:00	6:00
6:30	6:30	6:30	6:30
7:00	7:00	7:00	7:00
7:30	7:30	7:30	7:30
8:00	8:00	8:00	8:00
8:30	8:30	8:30	8:30
9:00	9:00	9:00	9:00
9:30	9:30	9:30	9:30
10:00	10:00	10:00	10:00
10:30	10:30	10:30	10:30
11:00	11:00	11:00	11:00
11:30	11:30	11:30	11:30
12:00	12:00	12:00	12:00
12:30	12:30	12:30	12:30

We are what we repeatedly do... Excellence, then is NOT an act, but a HABIT!	MON	TUES	WED	THURS	FRI	SAT	SUN
10 *BEFORE* **10 GRATITUDE**							
DECLARATIONS							
AUDIO							
READ							
FITNESS							
CONTACT 5 *BY* **5**							

THOUGHTS / IDEAS / VISIONS / DREAMS

THIS WEEK'S GOAL / FOCUS

WHAT DO I NEED TO...

STOP _____

_____

START _____

_____

CONTINUE _____

_____

QUOTE OF THE WEEK

"He who is not courageous enough to take risks will accomplish nothing in life."
MUHAMMAD ALI

DECLARATION OF THE WEEK

I have created unstoppable momentum worldwide that has my business growing bigger, faster, and better every single day!

WRITE YOUR OWN DECLARATIONS FOR THIS WEEK BELOW:

_____
_____
_____
_____
_____
_____
_____
_____
_____
_____
_____
_____
_____
_____
_____
_____
_____

MAXIMIZE YOUR LIFE PLANNER

MAKE IT HAPPEN **MONDAY** ☐	*TAKE ACTION* **TUESDAY** ☐	*WHATEVER IT TAKES* **WEDNESDAY** ☐
TODAY'S GOAL	TODAY'S GOAL	TODAY'S GOAL
5:00	5:00	5:00
5:30	5:30	5:30
6:00	6:00	6:00
6:30	6:30	6:30
7:00	7:00	7:00
7:30	7:30	7:30
8:00	8:00	8:00
8:30	8:30	8:30
9:00	9:00	9:00
9:30	9:30	9:30
10:00	10:00	10:00
10:30	10:30	10:30
11:00	11:00	11:00
11:30	11:30	11:30
12:00	12:00	12:00
12:30	12:30	12:30
1:00	1:00	1:00
1:30	1:30	1:30
2:00	2:00	2:00
2:30	2:30	2:30
3:00	3:00	3:00
3:30	3:30	3:30
4:00	4:00	4:00
4:30	4:30	4:30
5:00	5:00	5:00
5:30	5:30	5:30
6:00	6:00	6:00
6:30	6:30	6:30
7:00	7:00	7:00
7:30	7:30	7:30
8:00	8:00	8:00
8:30	8:30	8:30
9:00	9:00	9:00
9:30	9:30	9:30
10:00	10:00	10:00
10:30	10:30	10:30
11:00	11:00	11:00
11:30	11:30	11:30
12:00	12:00	12:00
12:30	12:30	12:30
PERSONAL TO-DO LIST	**WORK** TO-DO LIST	**FOLLOW UP** LIST
☐	☐	/
☐	☐	/
☐	☐	/
☐	☐	/
☐	☐	/
☐	☐	/
☐	☐	/
☐	☐	/
☐	☐	/

TURN IT UP **THURSDAY** ☐	FINISH STRONG **FRIDAY** ☐	STEP IT UP **SATURDAY** ☐	SOULFUL **SUNDAY** ☐
TODAY'S GOAL	TODAY'S GOAL	TODAY'S GOAL	TODAY'S GOAL

THURSDAY		FRIDAY		SATURDAY		SUNDAY	
5:00		5:00		5:00		5:00	
5:30		5:30		5:30		5:30	
6:00		6:00		6:00		6:00	
6:30		6:30		6:30		6:30	
7:00		7:00		7:00		7:00	
7:30		7:30		7:30		7:30	
8:00		8:00		8:00		8:00	
8:30		8:30		8:30		8:30	
9:00		9:00		9:00		9:00	
9:30		9:30		9:30		9:30	
10:00		10:00		10:00		10:00	
10:30		10:30		10:30		10:30	
11:00		11:00		11:00		11:00	
11:30		11:30		11:30		11:30	
12:00		12:00		12:00		12:00	
12:30		12:30		12:30		12:30	
1:00		1:00		1:00		1:00	
1:30		1:30		1:30		1:30	
2:00		2:00		2:00		2:00	
2:30		2:30		2:30		2:30	
3:00		3:00		3:00		3:00	
3:30		3:30		3:30		3:30	
4:00		4:00		4:00		4:00	
4:30		4:30		4:30		4:30	
5:00		5:00		5:00		5:00	
5:30		5:30		5:30		5:30	
6:00		6:00		6:00		6:00	
6:30		6:30		6:30		6:30	
7:00		7:00		7:00		7:00	
7:30		7:30		7:30		7:30	
8:00		8:00		8:00		8:00	
8:30		8:30		8:30		8:30	
9:00		9:00		9:00		9:00	
9:30		9:30		9:30		9:30	
10:00		10:00		10:00		10:00	
10:30		10:30		10:30		10:30	
11:00		11:00		11:00		11:00	
11:30		11:30		11:30		11:30	
12:00		12:00		12:00		12:00	
12:30		12:30		12:30		12:30	

We are what we repeatedly do... Excellence, then is NOT an act, but a HABIT!	MON	TUES	WED	THURS	FRI	SAT	SUN
10 *BEFORE* **10 GRATITUDE**							
DECLARATIONS							
AUDIO							
READ							
FITNESS							
CONTACT 5 *BY* **5**							

THOUGHTS / IDEAS / VISIONS / DREAMS

WEEK OF

/ / - / /

THIS WEEK'S GOAL / FOCUS

WHAT DO I NEED TO...

STOP _____

_____

START _____

_____

CONTINUE _____

_____

_____

QUOTE OF THE WEEK

"Your purpose in life is to find your voice and give it a voice."
STEPHEN COVEY

DECLARATION OF THE WEEK

I am blessed and highly favored.

WRITE YOUR OWN DECLARATIONS FOR THIS WEEK BELOW:

_____
_____
_____
_____
_____
_____
_____
_____
_____
_____
_____
_____
_____
_____
_____
_____
_____
_____
_____

MAKE IT HAPPEN **MONDAY** ☐	*TAKE ACTION* **TUESDAY** ☐	*WHATEVER IT TAKES* **WEDNESDAY** ☐
TODAY'S GOAL	TODAY'S GOAL	TODAY'S GOAL
5:00	5:00	5:00
5:30	5:30	5:30
6:00	6:00	6:00
6:30	6:30	6:30
7:00	7:00	7:00
7:30	7:30	7:30
8:00	8:00	8:00
8:30	8:30	8:30
9:00	9:00	9:00
9:30	9:30	9:30
10:00	10:00	10:00
10:30	10:30	10:30
11:00	11:00	11:00
11:30	11:30	11:30
12:00	12:00	12:00
12:30	12:30	12:30
1:00	1:00	1:00
1:30	1:30	1:30
2:00	2:00	2:00
2:30	2:30	2:30
3:00	3:00	3:00
3:30	3:30	3:30
4:00	4:00	4:00
4:30	4:30	4:30
5:00	5:00	5:00
5:30	5:30	5:30
6:00	6:00	6:00
6:30	6:30	6:30
7:00	7:00	7:00
7:30	7:30	7:30
8:00	8:00	8:00
8:30	8:30	8:30
9:00	9:00	9:00
9:30	9:30	9:30
10:00	10:00	10:00
10:30	10:30	10:30
11:00	11:00	11:00
11:30	11:30	11:30
12:00	12:00	12:00
12:30	12:30	12:30
PERSONAL TO-DO LIST	**WORK** TO-DO LIST	**FOLLOW UP** LIST
☐	☐	/
☐	☐	/
☐	☐	/
☐	☐	/
☐	☐	/
☐	☐	/
☐	☐	/
☐	☐	/

TURN IT UP
THURSDAY

FINISH STRONG
FRIDAY

STEP IT UP
SATURDAY

SOULFUL
SUNDAY

TODAY'S GOAL	TODAY'S GOAL	TODAY'S GOAL	TODAY'S GOAL
5:00	5:00	5:00	5:00
5:30	5:30	5:30	5:30
6:00	6:00	6:00	6:00
6:30	6:30	6:30	6:30
7:00	7:00	7:00	7:00
7:30	7:30	7:30	7:30
8:00	8:00	8:00	8:00
8:30	8:30	8:30	8:30
9:00	9:00	9:00	9:00
9:30	9:30	9:30	9:30
10:00	10:00	10:00	10:00
10:30	10:30	10:30	10:30
11:00	11:00	11:00	11:00
11:30	11:30	11:30	11:30
12:00	12:00	12:00	12:00
12:30	12:30	12:30	12:30
1:00	1:00	1:00	1:00
1:30	1:30	1:30	1:30
2:00	2:00	2:00	2:00
2:30	2:30	2:30	2:30
3:00	3:00	3:00	3:00
3:30	3:30	3:30	3:30
4:00	4:00	4:00	4:00
4:30	4:30	4:30	4:30
5:00	5:00	5:00	5:00
5:30	5:30	5:30	5:30
6:00	6:00	6:00	6:00
6:30	6:30	6:30	6:30
7:00	7:00	7:00	7:00
7:30	7:30	7:30	7:30
8:00	8:00	8:00	8:00
8:30	8:30	8:30	8:30
9:00	9:00	9:00	9:00
9:30	9:30	9:30	9:30
10:00	10:00	10:00	10:00
10:30	10:30	10:30	10:30
11:00	11:00	11:00	11:00
11:30	11:30	11:30	11:30
12:00	12:00	12:00	12:00
12:30	12:30	12:30	12:30

We are what we repeatedly do... Excellence, then is NOT an act, but a HABIT!	MON	TUES	WED	THURS	FRI	SAT	SUN
10 *BEFORE* 10 GRATITUDE							
DECLARATIONS							
AUDIO							
READ							
FITNESS							
CONTACT 5 *BY* 5							

THOUGHTS / IDEAS / VISIONS / DREAMS

WEEK OF
/   / - /   /

THIS WEEK'S GOAL / FOCUS

WHAT DO I NEED TO...

STOP _____

_____

START _____

_____

CONTINUE _____

_____

QUOTE OF THE WEEK

"I've failed over and over and over again in my life and that is why I succeed."
MICHAEL JORDAN

DECLARATION OF THE WEEK

I am rich with creative ideas.

WRITE YOUR OWN DECLARATIONS FOR THIS WEEK BELOW:

_____
_____
_____
_____
_____
_____
_____
_____
_____
_____
_____
_____
_____
_____
_____
_____

MAXIMIZE YOUR LIFE PLANNER

MAKE IT HAPPEN **MONDAY** ☐	TAKE ACTION **TUESDAY** ☐	WHATEVER IT TAKES **WEDNESDAY** ☐
TODAY'S GOAL	TODAY'S GOAL	TODAY'S GOAL
5:00	5:00	5:00
5:30	5:30	5:30
6:00	6:00	6:00
6:30	6:30	6:30
7:00	7:00	7:00
7:30	7:30	7:30
8:00	8:00	8:00
8:30	8:30	8:30
9:00	9:00	9:00
9:30	9:30	9:30
10:00	10:00	10:00
10:30	10:30	10:30
11:00	11:00	11:00
11:30	11:30	11:30
12:00	12:00	12:00
12:30	12:30	12:30
1:00	1:00	1:00
1:30	1:30	1:30
2:00	2:00	2:00
2:30	2:30	2:30
3:00	3:00	3:00
3:30	3:30	3:30
4:00	4:00	4:00
4:30	4:30	4:30
5:00	5:00	5:00
5:30	5:30	5:30
6:00	6:00	6:00
6:30	6:30	6:30
7:00	7:00	7:00
7:30	7:30	7:30
8:00	8:00	8:00
8:30	8:30	8:30
9:00	9:00	9:00
9:30	9:30	9:30
10:00	10:00	10:00
10:30	10:30	10:30
11:00	11:00	11:00
11:30	11:30	11:30
12:00	12:00	12:00
12:30	12:30	12:30
PERSONAL TO-DO LIST	**WORK** TO-DO LIST	**FOLLOW UP** LIST
☐	☐	/
☐	☐	/
☐	☐	/
☐	☐	/
☐	☐	/
☐	☐	/
☐	☐	/
☐	☐	/
☐	☐	/

TODAY'S GOAL	TODAY'S GOAL	TODAY'S GOAL	TODAY'S GOAL
5:00	5:00	5:00	5:00
5:30	5:30	5:30	5:30
6:00	6:00	6:00	6:00
6:30	6:30	6:30	6:30
7:00	7:00	7:00	7:00
7:30	7:30	7:30	7:30
8:00	8:00	8:00	8:00
8:30	8:30	8:30	8:30
9:00	9:00	9:00	9:00
9:30	9:30	9:30	9:30
10:00	10:00	10:00	10:00
10:30	10:30	10:30	10:30
11:00	11:00	11:00	11:00
11:30	11:30	11:30	11:30
12:00	12:00	12:00	12:00
12:30	12:30	12:30	12:30
1:00	1:00	1:00	1:00
1:30	1:30	1:30	1:30
2:00	2:00	2:00	2:00
2:30	2:30	2:30	2:30
3:00	3:00	3:00	3:00
3:30	3:30	3:30	3:30
4:00	4:00	4:00	4:00
4:30	4:30	4:30	4:30
5:00	5:00	5:00	5:00
5:30	5:30	5:30	5:30
6:00	6:00	6:00	6:00
6:30	6:30	6:30	6:30
7:00	7:00	7:00	7:00
7:30	7:30	7:30	7:30
8:00	8:00	8:00	8:00
8:30	8:30	8:30	8:30
9:00	9:00	9:00	9:00
9:30	9:30	9:30	9:30
10:00	10:00	10:00	10:00
10:30	10:30	10:30	10:30
11:00	11:00	11:00	11:00
11:30	11:30	11:30	11:30
12:00	12:00	12:00	12:00
12:30	12:30	12:30	12:30

We are what we repeatedly do... Excellence, then is NOT an act, but a HABIT!	MON	TUES	WED	THURS	FRI	SAT	SUN
10 *BEFORE* 10 GRATITUDE							
DECLARATIONS							
AUDIO							
READ							
FITNESS							
CONTACT 5 *BY* 5							

THOUGHTS / IDEAS / VISIONS / DREAMS

THIS WEEK'S GOAL / FOCUS

WHAT DO I NEED TO...

STOP _____

_____

START _____

_____

CONTINUE _____

_____

_____

QUOTE OF THE WEEK

"The easiest way to discover the purpose of an invention is to ask the creator of it. The same is true for discovering your life's purpose: Ask God."
RICK WARREN

DECLARATION OF THE WEEK

Unique and profitable opportunities fall in my lap.

WRITE YOUR OWN DECLARATIONS FOR THIS WEEK BELOW:

_____
_____
_____
_____
_____
_____
_____
_____
_____
_____
_____
_____
_____
_____
_____
_____
_____

MAXIMIZE YOUR LIFE PLANNER

MAKE IT HAPPEN **MONDAY** ☐	TAKE ACTION **TUESDAY** ☐	WHATEVER IT TAKES **WEDNESDAY** ☐
TODAY'S GOAL	TODAY'S GOAL	TODAY'S GOAL
5:00	5:00	5:00
5:30	5:30	5:30
6:00	6:00	6:00
6:30	6:30	6:30
7:00	7:00	7:00
7:30	7:30	7:30
8:00	8:00	8:00
8:30	8:30	8:30
9:00	9:00	9:00
9:30	9:30	9:30
10:00	10:00	10:00
10:30	10:30	10:30
11:00	11:00	11:00
11:30	11:30	11:30
12:00	12:00	12:00
12:30	12:30	12:30
1:00	1:00	1:00
1:30	1:30	1:30
2:00	2:00	2:00
2:30	2:30	2:30
3:00	3:00	3:00
3:30	3:30	3:30
4:00	4:00	4:00
4:30	4:30	4:30
5:00	5:00	5:00
5:30	5:30	5:30
6:00	6:00	6:00
6:30	6:30	6:30
7:00	7:00	7:00
7:30	7:30	7:30
8:00	8:00	8:00
8:30	8:30	8:30
9:00	9:00	9:00
9:30	9:30	9:30
10:00	10:00	10:00
10:30	10:30	10:30
11:00	11:00	11:00
11:30	11:30	11:30
12:00	12:00	12:00
12:30	12:30	12:30
PERSONAL TO-DO LIST	**WORK** TO-DO LIST	**FOLLOW UP** LIST
☐	☐	/
☐	☐	/
☐	☐	/
☐	☐	/
☐	☐	/
☐	☐	/
☐	☐	/
☐	☐	/
☐	☐	/

TODAY'S GOAL	TODAY'S GOAL	TODAY'S GOAL	TODAY'S GOAL
5:00	5:00	5:00	5:00
5:30	5:30	5:30	5:30
6:00	6:00	6:00	6:00
6:30	6:30	6:30	6:30
7:00	7:00	7:00	7:00
7:30	7:30	7:30	7:30
8:00	8:00	8:00	8:00
8:30	8:30	8:30	8:30
9:00	9:00	9:00	9:00
9:30	9:30	9:30	9:30
10:00	10:00	10:00	10:00
10:30	10:30	10:30	10:30
11:00	11:00	11:00	11:00
11:30	11:30	11:30	11:30
12:00	12:00	12:00	12:00
12:30	12:30	12:30	12:30
1:00	1:00	1:00	1:00
1:30	1:30	1:30	1:30
2:00	2:00	2:00	2:00
2:30	2:30	2:30	2:30
3:00	3:00	3:00	3:00
3:30	3:30	3:30	3:30
4:00	4:00	4:00	4:00
4:30	4:30	4:30	4:30
5:00	5:00	5:00	5:00
5:30	5:30	5:30	5:30
6:00	6:00	6:00	6:00
6:30	6:30	6:30	6:30
7:00	7:00	7:00	7:00
7:30	7:30	7:30	7:30
8:00	8:00	8:00	8:00
8:30	8:30	8:30	8:30
9:00	9:00	9:00	9:00
9:30	9:30	9:30	9:30
10:00	10:00	10:00	10:00
10:30	10:30	10:30	10:30
11:00	11:00	11:00	11:00
11:30	11:30	11:30	11:30
12:00	12:00	12:00	12:00
12:30	12:30	12:30	12:30

We are what we repeatedly do... Excellence, then is NOT an act, but a HABIT!

	MON	TUES	WED	THURS	FRI	SAT	SUN
10 BEFORE 10 GRATITUDE							
DECLARATIONS							
AUDIO							
READ							
FITNESS							
CONTACT 5 BY 5							

THOUGHTS / IDEAS / VISIONS / DREAMS

WEEK OF
/ / - / /

THIS WEEK'S GOAL / FOCUS

WHAT DO I NEED TO...

STOP _____

_____

START _____

_____

CONTINUE _____

_____

QUOTE OF THE WEEK

"We are all faced with a series of great opportunities brilliantly disguised as impossible situations."
CHUCK SWINDOLL

DECLARATION OF THE WEEK

I feel accomplished and overwhelmed with joy at the news that my dreams have become a reality!

WRITE YOUR OWN DECLARATIONS FOR THIS WEEK BELOW:

_____
_____
_____
_____
_____
_____
_____
_____
_____
_____
_____
_____
_____
_____
_____
_____
_____

MAXIMIZE
YOUR LIFE
P L A N N E R

	MAKE IT HAPPEN **MONDAY** ☐	TAKE ACTION **TUESDAY** ☐	WHATEVER IT TAKES **WEDNESDAY** ☐
	TODAY'S GOAL	TODAY'S GOAL	TODAY'S GOAL
5:00			
5:30			
6:00			
6:30			
7:00			
7:30			
8:00			
8:30			
9:00			
9:30			
10:00			
10:30			
11:00			
11:30			
12:00			
12:30			
1:00			
1:30			
2:00			
2:30			
3:00			
3:30			
4:00			
4:30			
5:00			
5:30			
6:00			
6:30			
7:00			
7:30			
8:00			
8:30			
9:00			
9:30			
10:00			
10:30			
11:00			
11:30			
12:00			
12:30			

PERSONAL TO-DO LIST	**WORK** TO-DO LIST	**FOLLOW UP** LIST
☐	☐	/
☐	☐	/
☐	☐	/
☐	☐	/
☐	☐	/
☐	☐	/
☐	☐	/
☐	☐	/
☐	☐	/

THURSDAY TODAY'S GOAL	FRIDAY TODAY'S GOAL	SATURDAY TODAY'S GOAL	SUNDAY TODAY'S GOAL
5:00	5:00	5:00	5:00
5:30	5:30	5:30	5:30
6:00	6:00	6:00	6:00
6:30	6:30	6:30	6:30
7:00	7:00	7:00	7:00
7:30	7:30	7:30	7:30
8:00	8:00	8:00	8:00
8:30	8:30	8:30	8:30
9:00	9:00	9:00	9:00
9:30	9:30	9:30	9:30
10:00	10:00	10:00	10:00
10:30	10:30	10:30	10:30
11:00	11:00	11:00	11:00
11:30	11:30	11:30	11:30
12:00	12:00	12:00	12:00
12:30	12:30	12:30	12:30
1:00	1:00	1:00	1:00
1:30	1:30	1:30	1:30
2:00	2:00	2:00	2:00
2:30	2:30	2:30	2:30
3:00	3:00	3:00	3:00
3:30	3:30	3:30	3:30
4:00	4:00	4:00	4:00
4:30	4:30	4:30	4:30
5:00	5:00	5:00	5:00
5:30	5:30	5:30	5:30
6:00	6:00	6:00	6:00
6:30	6:30	6:30	6:30
7:00	7:00	7:00	7:00
7:30	7:30	7:30	7:30
8:00	8:00	8:00	8:00
8:30	8:30	8:30	8:30
9:00	9:00	9:00	9:00
9:30	9:30	9:30	9:30
10:00	10:00	10:00	10:00
10:30	10:30	10:30	10:30
11:00	11:00	11:00	11:00
11:30	11:30	11:30	11:30
12:00	12:00	12:00	12:00
12:30	12:30	12:30	12:30

We are what we repeatedly do... Excellence, then is NOT an act, but a HABIT!	MON	TUES	WED	THURS	FRI	SAT	SUN
10 *BEFORE* 10 GRATITUDE							
DECLARATIONS							
AUDIO							
READ							
FITNESS							
CONTACT 5 *BY* 5							

THOUGHTS / IDEAS / VISIONS / DREAMS

WEEK OF
/ / - / /

THIS WEEK'S GOAL / FOCUS

WHAT DO I NEED TO...

STOP _____

_____

START _____

_____

CONTINUE _____

_____

QUOTE OF THE WEEK
"To live is the rarest thing in the world. Most people exist, that is all."
OSCAR WILDE

DECLARATION OF THE WEEK
I am happy and honored to be recognized and celebrated for my recent achievements.

WRITE YOUR OWN DECLARATIONS FOR THIS WEEK BELOW:

_____
_____
_____
_____
_____
_____
_____
_____
_____
_____
_____
_____
_____
_____
_____
_____

MAXIMIZE YOUR LIFE PLANNER

MAKE IT HAPPEN **MONDAY**	*TAKE ACTION* **TUESDAY**	*WHATEVER IT TAKES* **WEDNESDAY**
TODAY'S GOAL	TODAY'S GOAL	TODAY'S GOAL
5:00	5:00	5:00
5:30	5:30	5:30
6:00	6:00	6:00
6:30	6:30	6:30
7:00	7:00	7:00
7:30	7:30	7:30
8:00	8:00	8:00
8:30	8:30	8:30
9:00	9:00	9:00
9:30	9:30	9:30
10:00	10:00	10:00
10:30	10:30	10:30
11:00	11:00	11:00
11:30	11:30	11:30
12:00	12:00	12:00
12:30	12:30	12:30
1:00	1:00	1:00
1:30	1:30	1:30
2:00	2:00	2:00
2:30	2:30	2:30
3:00	3:00	3:00
3:30	3:30	3:30
4:00	4:00	4:00
4:30	4:30	4:30
5:00	5:00	5:00
5:30	5:30	5:30
6:00	6:00	6:00
6:30	6:30	6:30
7:00	7:00	7:00
7:30	7:30	7:30
8:00	8:00	8:00
8:30	8:30	8:30
9:00	9:00	9:00
9:30	9:30	9:30
10:00	10:00	10:00
10:30	10:30	10:30
11:00	11:00	11:00
11:30	11:30	11:30
12:00	12:00	12:00
12:30	12:30	12:30
PERSONAL TO-DO LIST	**WORK** TO-DO LIST	**FOLLOW UP** LIST
☐	☐	/
☐	☐	/
☐	☐	/
☐	☐	/
☐	☐	/
☐	☐	/
☐	☐	/
☐	☐	/
☐	☐	/

TURN IT UP
THURSDAY ☐
FINISH STRONG
FRIDAY ☐
STEP IT UP
SATURDAY ☐
SOULFUL
SUNDAY ☐

THURSDAY TODAY'S GOAL	FRIDAY TODAY'S GOAL	SATURDAY TODAY'S GOAL	SUNDAY TODAY'S GOAL
5:00	5:00	5:00	5:00
5:30	5:30	5:30	5:30
6:00	6:00	6:00	6:00
6:30	6:30	6:30	6:30
7:00	7:00	7:00	7:00
7:30	7:30	7:30	7:30
8:00	8:00	8:00	8:00
8:30	8:30	8:30	8:30
9:00	9:00	9:00	9:00
9:30	9:30	9:30	9:30
10:00	10:00	10:00	10:00
10:30	10:30	10:30	10:30
11:00	11:00	11:00	11:00
11:30	11:30	11:30	11:30
12:00	12:00	12:00	12:00
12:30	12:30	12:30	12:30
1:00	1:00	1:00	1:00
1:30	1:30	1:30	1:30
2:00	2:00	2:00	2:00
2:30	2:30	2:30	2:30
3:00	3:00	3:00	3:00
3:30	3:30	3:30	3:30
4:00	4:00	4:00	4:00
4:30	4:30	4:30	4:30
5:00	5:00	5:00	5:00
5:30	5:30	5:30	5:30
6:00	6:00	6:00	6:00
6:30	6:30	6:30	6:30
7:00	7:00	7:00	7:00
7:30	7:30	7:30	7:30
8:00	8:00	8:00	8:00
8:30	8:30	8:30	8:30
9:00	9:00	9:00	9:00
9:30	9:30	9:30	9:30
10:00	10:00	10:00	10:00
10:30	10:30	10:30	10:30
11:00	11:00	11:00	11:00
11:30	11:30	11:30	11:30
12:00	12:00	12:00	12:00
12:30	12:30	12:30	12:30

We are what we repeatedly do... Excellence, then is NOT an act, but a HABIT!

	MON	TUES	WED	THURS	FRI	SAT	SUN
10 *BEFORE* 10 GRATITUDE							
DECLARATIONS							
AUDIO							
READ							
FITNESS							
CONTACT 5 *BY* 5							

THOUGHTS / IDEAS / VISIONS / DREAMS

WEEK OF
/ __ - / __ / __

THIS WEEK'S GOAL / FOCUS

WHAT DO I NEED TO...

STOP _____
_____

START _____
_____

CONTINUE _____
_____

QUOTE OF THE WEEK
"The two most important days in your life are the day you are born and the day you find out why."
MARK TWAIN

DECLARATION OF THE WEEK
Step by step, and rep by rep, I am creating my ideal body.

WRITE YOUR OWN DECLARATIONS FOR THIS WEEK BELOW:
_____
_____
_____
_____
_____
_____
_____
_____
_____
_____
_____
_____
_____
_____
_____
_____
_____

MAXIMIZE YOUR LIFE
P L A N N E R

MAKE IT HAPPEN MONDAY	TAKE ACTION TUESDAY	WHATEVER IT TAKES WEDNESDAY
TODAY'S GOAL	TODAY'S GOAL	TODAY'S GOAL
5:00	5:00	5:00
5:30	5:30	5:30
6:00	6:00	6:00
6:30	6:30	6:30
7:00	7:00	7:00
7:30	7:30	7:30
8:00	8:00	8:00
8:30	8:30	8:30
9:00	9:00	9:00
9:30	9:30	9:30
10:00	10:00	10:00
10:30	10:30	10:30
11:00	11:00	11:00
11:30	11:30	11:30
12:00	12:00	12:00
12:30	12:30	12:30
1:00	1:00	1:00
1:30	1:30	1:30
2:00	2:00	2:00
2:30	2:30	2:30
3:00	3:00	3:00
3:30	3:30	3:30
4:00	4:00	4:00
4:30	4:30	4:30
5:00	5:00	5:00
5:30	5:30	5:30
6:00	6:00	6:00
6:30	6:30	6:30
7:00	7:00	7:00
7:30	7:30	7:30
8:00	8:00	8:00
8:30	8:30	8:30
9:00	9:00	9:00
9:30	9:30	9:30
10:00	10:00	10:00
10:30	10:30	10:30
11:00	11:00	11:00
11:30	11:30	11:30
12:00	12:00	12:00
12:30	12:30	12:30
PERSONAL TO-DO LIST	**WORK** TO-DO LIST	**FOLLOW UP** LIST
☐	☐	/
☐	☐	/
☐	☐	/
☐	☐	/
☐	☐	/
☐	☐	/
☐	☐	/
☐	☐	/
☐	☐	/

TURN IT UP **THURSDAY** ☐	FINISH STRONG **FRIDAY** ☐	STEP IT UP **SATURDAY** ☐	SOULFUL **SUNDAY** ☐
TODAY'S GOAL	TODAY'S GOAL	TODAY'S GOAL	TODAY'S GOAL

THURSDAY	FRIDAY	SATURDAY	SUNDAY
5:00	5:00	5:00	5:00
5:30	5:30	5:30	5:30
6:00	6:00	6:00	6:00
6:30	6:30	6:30	6:30
7:00	7:00	7:00	7:00
7:30	7:30	7:30	7:30
8:00	8:00	8:00	8:00
8:30	8:30	8:30	8:30
9:00	9:00	9:00	9:00
9:30	9:30	9:30	9:30
10:00	10:00	10:00	10:00
10:30	10:30	10:30	10:30
11:00	11:00	11:00	11:00
11:30	11:30	11:30	11:30
12:00	12:00	12:00	12:00
12:30	12:30	12:30	12:30
1:00	1:00	1:00	1:00
1:30	1:30	1:30	1:30
2:00	2:00	2:00	2:00
2:30	2:30	2:30	2:30
3:00	3:00	3:00	3:00
3:30	3:30	3:30	3:30
4:00	4:00	4:00	4:00
4:30	4:30	4:30	4:30
5:00	5:00	5:00	5:00
5:30	5:30	5:30	5:30
6:00	6:00	6:00	6:00
6:30	6:30	6:30	6:30
7:00	7:00	7:00	7:00
7:30	7:30	7:30	7:30
8:00	8:00	8:00	8:00
8:30	8:30	8:30	8:30
9:00	9:00	9:00	9:00
9:30	9:30	9:30	9:30
10:00	10:00	10:00	10:00
10:30	10:30	10:30	10:30
11:00	11:00	11:00	11:00
11:30	11:30	11:30	11:30
12:00	12:00	12:00	12:00
12:30	12:30	12:30	12:30

We are what we repeatedly do... Excellence, then is NOT an act, but a HABIT!	MON	TUES	WED	THURS	FRI	SAT	SUN
10 *BEFORE* **10 GRATITUDE**							
DECLARATIONS							
AUDIO							
READ							
FITNESS							
CONTACT 5 *BY* **5**							

THOUGHTS / IDEAS / VISIONS / DREAMS

THIS WEEK'S GOAL / FOCUS

WHAT DO I NEED TO...

STOP _____

_____

START _____

_____

CONTINUE _____

_____

_____

QUOTE OF THE WEEK

"Don't live the same year 75 times and call it a life"
ROBIN SHARMA

DECLARATION OF THE WEEK

Everything I do leads to something positive.

WRITE YOUR OWN DECLARATIONS FOR THIS WEEK BELOW:

_____
_____
_____
_____
_____
_____
_____
_____
_____
_____
_____
_____
_____
_____
_____
_____
_____
_____
_____
_____

MAXIMIZE YOUR LIFE PLANNER

MAKE IT HAPPEN **MONDAY** ☐	*TAKE ACTION* **TUESDAY** ☐	*WHATEVER IT TAKES* **WEDNESDAY** ☐
TODAY'S GOAL	TODAY'S GOAL	TODAY'S GOAL
5:00	5:00	5:00
5:30	5:30	5:30
6:00	6:00	6:00
6:30	6:30	6:30
7:00	7:00	7:00
7:30	7:30	7:30
8:00	8:00	8:00
8:30	8:30	8:30
9:00	9:00	9:00
9:30	9:30	9:30
10:00	10:00	10:00
10:30	10:30	10:30
11:00	11:00	11:00
11:30	11:30	11:30
12:00	12:00	12:00
12:30	12:30	12:30
1:00	1:00	1:00
1:30	1:30	1:30
2:00	2:00	2:00
2:30	2:30	2:30
3:00	3:00	3:00
3:30	3:30	3:30
4:00	4:00	4:00
4:30	4:30	4:30
5:00	5:00	5:00
5:30	5:30	5:30
6:00	6:00	6:00
6:30	6:30	6:30
7:00	7:00	7:00
7:30	7:30	7:30
8:00	8:00	8:00
8:30	8:30	8:30
9:00	9:00	9:00
9:30	9:30	9:30
10:00	10:00	10:00
10:30	10:30	10:30
11:00	11:00	11:00
11:30	11:30	11:30
12:00	12:00	12:00
12:30	12:30	12:30
PERSONAL TO-DO LIST	**WORK** TO-DO LIST	**FOLLOW UP** LIST
☐	☐	/
☐	☐	/
☐	☐	/
☐	☐	/
☐	☐	/
☐	☐	/
☐	☐	/
☐	☐	/
☐	☐	/

THURSDAY TODAY'S GOAL	FRIDAY TODAY'S GOAL	SATURDAY TODAY'S GOAL	SUNDAY TODAY'S GOAL
5:00	5:00	5:00	5:00
5:30	5:30	5:30	5:30
6:00	6:00	6:00	6:00
6:30	6:30	6:30	6:30
7:00	7:00	7:00	7:00
7:30	7:30	7:30	7:30
8:00	8:00	8:00	8:00
8:30	8:30	8:30	8:30
9:00	9:00	9:00	9:00
9:30	9:30	9:30	9:30
10:00	10:00	10:00	10:00
10:30	10:30	10:30	10:30
11:00	11:00	11:00	11:00
11:30	11:30	11:30	11:30
12:00	12:00	12:00	12:00
12:30	12:30	12:30	12:30
1:00	1:00	1:00	1:00
1:30	1:30	1:30	1:30
2:00	2:00	2:00	2:00
2:30	2:30	2:30	2:30
3:00	3:00	3:00	3:00
3:30	3:30	3:30	3:30
4:00	4:00	4:00	4:00
4:30	4:30	4:30	4:30
5:00	5:00	5:00	5:00
5:30	5:30	5:30	5:30
6:00	6:00	6:00	6:00
6:30	6:30	6:30	6:30
7:00	7:00	7:00	7:00
7:30	7:30	7:30	7:30
8:00	8:00	8:00	8:00
8:30	8:30	8:30	8:30
9:00	9:00	9:00	9:00
9:30	9:30	9:30	9:30
10:00	10:00	10:00	10:00
10:30	10:30	10:30	10:30
11:00	11:00	11:00	11:00
11:30	11:30	11:30	11:30
12:00	12:00	12:00	12:00
12:30	12:30	12:30	12:30

We are what we repeatedly do... Excellence, then is NOT an act, but a HABIT!

	MON	TUES	WED	THURS	FRI	SAT	SUN
10 BEFORE 10 GRATITUDE							
DECLARATIONS							
AUDIO							
READ							
FITNESS							
CONTACT 5 BY 5							

THOUGHTS / IDEAS / VISIONS / DREAMS

WEEK OF
/ / - / /

THIS WEEK'S GOAL / FOCUS

WHAT DO I NEED TO...

STOP _____

_____

START _____

_____

CONTINUE _____

_____

_____

QUOTE OF THE WEEK

"All men dream, but not equally. Those who dream by night in the dusty recesses of their minds, wake in the day to find that all was vanity. But the dreamers of the day are dangerous men for they may act their dream with open eyes and make it possible."

T.E. LAWRENCE

DECLARATION OF THE WEEK

I have all that I need to make this a great day of my life.

WRITE YOUR OWN DECLARATIONS FOR THIS WEEK BELOW:

_____
_____
_____
_____
_____
_____
_____
_____
_____
_____
_____
_____

MAXIMIZE
YOUR LIFE
P L A N N E R

	MAKE IT HAPPEN MONDAY	TAKE ACTION TUESDAY	WHATEVER IT TAKES WEDNESDAY
	TODAY'S GOAL	TODAY'S GOAL	TODAY'S GOAL
5:00			
5:30			
6:00			
6:30			
7:00			
7:30			
8:00			
8:30			
9:00			
9:30			
10:00			
10:30			
11:00			
11:30			
12:00			
12:30			
1:00			
1:30			
2:00			
2:30			
3:00			
3:30			
4:00			
4:30			
5:00			
5:30			
6:00			
6:30			
7:00			
7:30			
8:00			
8:30			
9:00			
9:30			
10:00			
10:30			
11:00			
11:30			
12:00			
12:30			

PERSONAL TO-DO LIST	WORK TO-DO LIST	FOLLOW UP LIST
☐	☐	/
☐	☐	/
☐	☐	/
☐	☐	/
☐	☐	/
☐	☐	/
☐	☐	/
☐	☐	/
☐	☐	/

TURN IT UP THURSDAY ☐	FINISH STRONG FRIDAY ☐	STEP IT UP SATURDAY ☐	SOULFUL SUNDAY ☐
TODAY'S GOAL	TODAY'S GOAL	TODAY'S GOAL	TODAY'S GOAL

Thursday	Friday	Saturday	Sunday
5:00	5:00	5:00	5:00
5:30	5:30	5:30	5:30
6:00	6:00	6:00	6:00
6:30	6:30	6:30	6:30
7:00	7:00	7:00	7:00
7:30	7:30	7:30	7:30
8:00	8:00	8:00	8:00
8:30	8:30	8:30	8:30
9:00	9:00	9:00	9:00
9:30	9:30	9:30	9:30
10:00	10:00	10:00	10:00
10:30	10:30	10:30	10:30
11:00	11:00	11:00	11:00
11:30	11:30	11:30	11:30
12:00	12:00	12:00	12:00
12:30	12:30	12:30	12:30
1:00	1:00	1:00	1:00
1:30	1:30	1:30	1:30
2:00	2:00	2:00	2:00
2:30	2:30	2:30	2:30
3:00	3:00	3:00	3:00
3:30	3:30	3:30	3:30
4:00	4:00	4:00	4:00
4:30	4:30	4:30	4:30
5:00	5:00	5:00	5:00
5:30	5:30	5:30	5:30
6:00	6:00	6:00	6:00
6:30	6:30	6:30	6:30
7:00	7:00	7:00	7:00
7:30	7:30	7:30	7:30
8:00	8:00	8:00	8:00
8:30	8:30	8:30	8:30
9:00	9:00	9:00	9:00
9:30	9:30	9:30	9:30
10:00	10:00	10:00	10:00
10:30	10:30	10:30	10:30
11:00	11:00	11:00	11:00
11:30	11:30	11:30	11:30
12:00	12:00	12:00	12:00
12:30	12:30	12:30	12:30

We are what we repeatedly do... Excellence, then is NOT an act, but a HABIT!	MON	TUES	WED	THURS	FRI	SAT	SUN
10 BEFORE 10 GRATITUDE							
DECLARATIONS							
AUDIO							
READ							
FITNESS							
CONTACT 5 BY 5							

THOUGHTS / IDEAS / VISIONS / DREAMS

WEEK OF
/ / - / /

THIS WEEK'S GOAL / FOCUS

WHAT DO I NEED TO...

STOP _____

_____

START _____

_____

CONTINUE _____

_____

_____

QUOTE OF THE WEEK

"One day you will wake up and there won't be any more time to do the things you've always wanted. Do it now."
PAOLO COELHO

DECLARATION OF THE WEEK

I am so grateful to be earning a passive income from multiple business ventures and investments.

WRITE YOUR OWN DECLARATIONS FOR THIS WEEK BELOW:

_____
_____
_____
_____
_____
_____
_____
_____
_____
_____
_____
_____
_____
_____

MAXIMIZE YOUR LIFE
P L A N N E R

MAKE IT HAPPEN MONDAY	TAKE ACTION TUESDAY	WHATEVER IT TAKES WEDNESDAY
TODAY'S GOAL	TODAY'S GOAL	TODAY'S GOAL
5:00	5:00	5:00
5:30	5:30	5:30
6:00	6:00	6:00
6:30	6:30	6:30
7:00	7:00	7:00
7:30	7:30	7:30
8:00	8:00	8:00
8:30	8:30	8:30
9:00	9:00	9:00
9:30	9:30	9:30
10:00	10:00	10:00
10:30	10:30	10:30
11:00	11:00	11:00
11:30	11:30	11:30
12:00	12:00	12:00
12:30	12:30	12:30
1:00	1:00	1:00
1:30	1:30	1:30
2:00	2:00	2:00
2:30	2:30	2:30
3:00	3:00	3:00
3:30	3:30	3:30
4:00	4:00	4:00
4:30	4:30	4:30
5:00	5:00	5:00
5:30	5:30	5:30
6:00	6:00	6:00
6:30	6:30	6:30
7:00	7:00	7:00
7:30	7:30	7:30
8:00	8:00	8:00
8:30	8:30	8:30
9:00	9:00	9:00
9:30	9:30	9:30
10:00	10:00	10:00
10:30	10:30	10:30
11:00	11:00	11:00
11:30	11:30	11:30
12:00	12:00	12:00
12:30	12:30	12:30
PERSONAL TO-DO LIST	**WORK** TO-DO LIST	**FOLLOW UP** LIST
☐	☐	/
☐	☐	/
☐	☐	/
☐	☐	/
☐	☐	/
☐	☐	/
☐	☐	/
☐	☐	/
☐	☐	/

TODAY'S GOAL	TODAY'S GOAL	TODAY'S GOAL	TODAY'S GOAL
5:00	5:00	5:00	5:00
5:30	5:30	5:30	5:30
6:00	6:00	6:00	6:00
6:30	6:30	6:30	6:30
7:00	7:00	7:00	7:00
7:30	7:30	7:30	7:30
8:00	8:00	8:00	8:00
8:30	8:30	8:30	8:30
9:00	9:00	9:00	9:00
9:30	9:30	9:30	9:30
10:00	10:00	10:00	10:00
10:30	10:30	10:30	10:30
11:00	11:00	11:00	11:00
11:30	11:30	11:30	11:30
12:00	12:00	12:00	12:00
12:30	12:30	12:30	12:30
1:00	1:00	1:00	1:00
1:30	1:30	1:30	1:30
2:00	2:00	2:00	2:00
2:30	2:30	2:30	2:30
3:00	3:00	3:00	3:00
3:30	3:30	3:30	3:30
4:00	4:00	4:00	4:00
4:30	4:30	4:30	4:30
5:00	5:00	5:00	5:00
5:30	5:30	5:30	5:30
6:00	6:00	6:00	6:00
6:30	6:30	6:30	6:30
7:00	7:00	7:00	7:00
7:30	7:30	7:30	7:30
8:00	8:00	8:00	8:00
8:30	8:30	8:30	8:30
9:00	9:00	9:00	9:00
9:30	9:30	9:30	9:30
10:00	10:00	10:00	10:00
10:30	10:30	10:30	10:30
11:00	11:00	11:00	11:00
11:30	11:30	11:30	11:30
12:00	12:00	12:00	12:00
12:30	12:30	12:30	12:30

We are what we repeatedly do... Excellence, then is NOT an act, but a HABIT!	MON	TUES	WED	THURS	FRI	SAT	SUN
10 *BEFORE* 10 GRATITUDE							
DECLARATIONS							
AUDIO							
READ							
FITNESS							
CONTACT 5 *BY* 5							

THOUGHTS / IDEAS / VISIONS / DREAMS

WEEK OF

/ / - / /

THIS WEEK'S GOAL / FOCUS

WHAT DO I NEED TO...

STOP _____

_____

START _____

_____

CONTINUE _____

_____

QUOTE OF THE WEEK

"If you believe, all things are possible to him who believes."
JESUS

DECLARATION OF THE WEEK

My life matters and the world is a better place because of my effort, contribution, and service.

WRITE YOUR OWN DECLARATIONS FOR THIS WEEK BELOW:

_____
_____
_____
_____
_____
_____
_____
_____
_____
_____
_____
_____
_____
_____
_____
_____
_____
_____
_____
_____
_____
_____

MAXIMIZE YOUR LIFE PLANNER

MAKE IT HAPPEN **MONDAY** ☐	TAKE ACTION **TUESDAY** ☐	WHATEVER IT TAKES **WEDNESDAY** ☐
TODAY'S GOAL	TODAY'S GOAL	TODAY'S GOAL
5:00	5:00	5:00
5:30	5:30	5:30
6:00	6:00	6:00
6:30	6:30	6:30
7:00	7:00	7:00
7:30	7:30	7:30
8:00	8:00	8:00
8:30	8:30	8:30
9:00	9:00	9:00
9:30	9:30	9:30
10:00	10:00	10:00
10:30	10:30	10:30
11:00	11:00	11:00
11:30	11:30	11:30
12:00	12:00	12:00
12:30	12:30	12:30
1:00	1:00	1:00
1:30	1:30	1:30
2:00	2:00	2:00
2:30	2:30	2:30
3:00	3:00	3:00
3:30	3:30	3:30
4:00	4:00	4:00
4:30	4:30	4:30
5:00	5:00	5:00
5:30	5:30	5:30
6:00	6:00	6:00
6:30	6:30	6:30
7:00	7:00	7:00
7:30	7:30	7:30
8:00	8:00	8:00
8:30	8:30	8:30
9:00	9:00	9:00
9:30	9:30	9:30
10:00	10:00	10:00
10:30	10:30	10:30
11:00	11:00	11:00
11:30	11:30	11:30
12:00	12:00	12:00
12:30	12:30	12:30
PERSONAL TO-DO LIST	**WORK** TO-DO LIST	**FOLLOW UP** LIST
☐	☐	/
☐	☐	/
☐	☐	/
☐	☐	/
☐	☐	/
☐	☐	/
☐	☐	/
☐	☐	/
☐	☐	/

THURSDAY — TODAY'S GOAL

Time	
5:00	
5:30	
6:00	
6:30	
7:00	
7:30	
8:00	
8:30	
9:00	
9:30	
10:00	
10:30	
11:00	
11:30	
12:00	
12:30	
1:00	
1:30	
2:00	
2:30	
3:00	
3:30	
4:00	
4:30	
5:00	
5:30	
6:00	
6:30	
7:00	
7:30	
8:00	
8:30	
9:00	
9:30	
10:00	
10:30	
11:00	
11:30	
12:00	
12:30	

FRIDAY — TODAY'S GOAL

Time	
5:00	
5:30	
6:00	
6:30	
7:00	
7:30	
8:00	
8:30	
9:00	
9:30	
10:00	
10:30	
11:00	
11:30	
12:00	
12:30	
1:00	
1:30	
2:00	
2:30	
3:00	
3:30	
4:00	
4:30	
5:00	
5:30	
6:00	
6:30	
7:00	
7:30	
8:00	
8:30	
9:00	
9:30	
10:00	
10:30	
11:00	
11:30	
12:00	
12:30	

SATURDAY — TODAY'S GOAL

Time	
5:00	
5:30	
6:00	
6:30	
7:00	
7:30	
8:00	
8:30	
9:00	
9:30	
10:00	
10:30	
11:00	
11:30	
12:00	
12:30	
1:00	
1:30	
2:00	
2:30	
3:00	
3:30	
4:00	
4:30	
5:00	
5:30	
6:00	
6:30	
7:00	
7:30	
8:00	
8:30	
9:00	
9:30	
10:00	
10:30	
11:00	
11:30	
12:00	
12:30	

SUNDAY — TODAY'S GOAL

Time	
5:00	
5:30	
6:00	
6:30	
7:00	
7:30	
8:00	
8:30	
9:00	
9:30	
10:00	
10:30	
11:00	
11:30	
12:00	
12:30	
1:00	
1:30	
2:00	
2:30	
3:00	
3:30	
4:00	
4:30	
5:00	
5:30	
6:00	
6:30	
7:00	
7:30	
8:00	
8:30	
9:00	
9:30	
10:00	
10:30	
11:00	
11:30	
12:00	
12:30	

We are what we repeatedly do... Excellence, then is NOT an act, but a HABIT!

	MON	TUES	WED	THURS	FRI	SAT	SUN
10 *BEFORE* 10 GRATITUDE							
DECLARATIONS							
AUDIO							
READ							
FITNESS							
CONTACT 5 *BY* 5							

THOUGHTS / IDEAS / VISIONS / DREAMS

Time to Order a NEW Planner? www.MaximizeYourLifePlanner.com

Your thoughts are the foundation of your reality, so make them powerful and uplifting.

A dream becomes a goal when action is taken toward its achievement.

Ideas are the sparks that ignite progress and change in the world.

Dreams are the whispers from God, inviting you to explore the infinite possibilities of your soul.

The power of your imagination can transport you to new worlds and unlock limitless potential.

The more ideas you generate, the more chances you have of finding a great one.

Your ideas have the potential to change the course of history and make the world a better place.

Imagination is more important than knowledge, for knowledge is limited while imagination encircles the world.

Great ideas come from a place of openness and curiosity, where anything is possible.

Dreams are the catalysts for growth and expansion, urging us to break free from our limitations.

Creativity is the ability to see what everyone else has seen, and think what no one else has thought.

Imagination is not a talent, it's a muscle that can be strengthened with practice.

Your thoughts can either be your ally or your enemy… choose wisely.

The best way to predict the future is to create it.

Imagination is the force that drives innovation.

Creativity is the freedom to express oneself without fear of judgment.

Your thoughts can create a positive ripple effect, inspiring others to do the same.

You don't need to have a perfect idea to start, just a willingness to explore and create.

Inspiration can come from anywhere… keep an open mind and be ready to catch it when it arrives.

Your thoughts have the power to shift the energy of the world… starting with your own.

Don't be afraid to break the rules and think outside the box... sometimes the best ideas are the ones that defy convention.

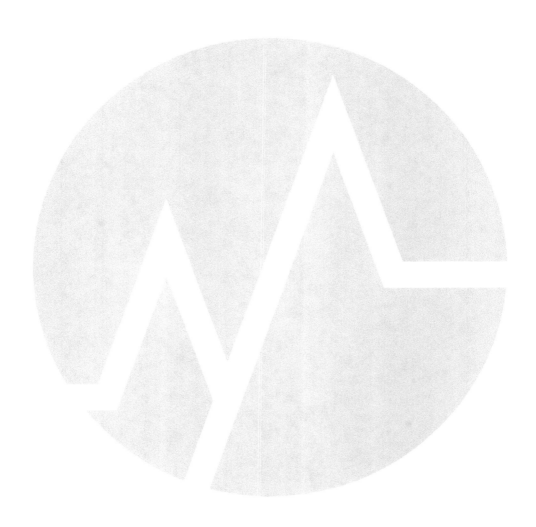

Brainstorming is a way to harness the power of your subconscious mind and tap into your intuition.

Your thoughts can either limit your potential or unlock it... choose wisely.

The best ideas often come from a place of passion and authenticity.

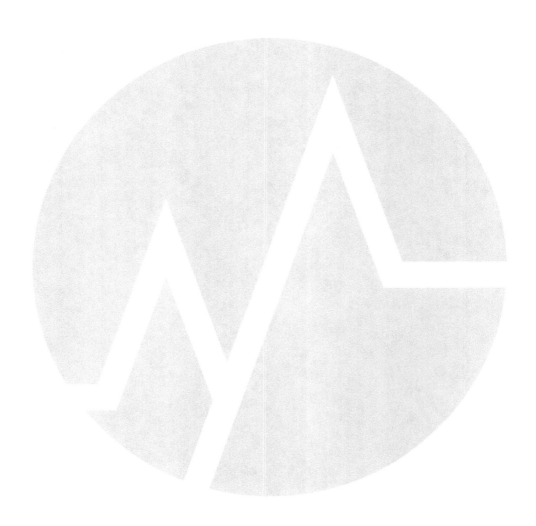

ABOUT THE CREATOR

Maximo Lora is a faith-driven, creative, and energetic leader with a passion to serve the person who he once was… an employee working 50-60 hours a week, with an aching desire to discover his God-given purpose and live a better quality lifestyle. Now, as a leadership and business coach, Maximo works with entrepreneurs and business owners who want to maximize their potential and make an empowering impact on the world.

With over twenty years of marketing, graphics, and communication experience, Maximo knows how to get a message across to not only his clients but to their customers as well. This also allows him to connect with a crowd and provide principles so that others can effectively do the same.

Maximo's down-to-earth personality and sense of humor leads audiences to not only relate, but also laugh while they learn. He engages groups from the moment he steps in front of them, and leaves them with a focused mindset as well as a clear mission towards their goals and dreams. Maximo is dedicated to serve people and impact the world through his leadership and business experience. He is passionate about inspiring those around him to grow, prosper, and live life to the max!

When not speaking or training, Maximo can be found traveling the world and tasting different international dishes with his wife and foodie partner Karen.

Find Maximo online at **www.MaximoLora.com**